Contents

Choose a strong idea before you write.
It's easier to write about what you know.

A. Read each paragraph about a city. Fix the names of places that need a capital letter. Then answer the questions.

Bevington
by Jacob

bevington is a great town. At Lake jasper, you can rent a boat and have a cookout on the shore. There are also many places to eat a cold ice-cream cone on a hot day. The people are friendly in town. They love showing visitors around.

New Delway
by Michael

New delway is in Monitor county. Highway 4 goes there. My friend went there once. There is a gas station. I heard they're getting a new grocery store.

1. Which writer has probably been to the town he wrote about? Give one reason why.

   ____

   ____

2. Which writer has more interesting things to say about his topic?

   ____

B. Answer the questions with ideas you can write about.

1. Name a place you've visited. ____

2. What is one interesting thing you can say about that place?

   ____

Your purpose is the reason you're writing.
A strong idea is one that fits your purpose.

A. Begley Bookstore gave Emily's class free books. Her class decided to write thank-you letters. Read Emily's letter and answer the questions. Fix the names that need a capital letter.

> Dear Begley Bookstore,
>
> Leonard Saves the Day was the book I got. Leonard is the main character. He is a bear that rides a scooter around town. He helps people. In the end, leonard saves mayor Jones from Mr. badman, an evil wizard.
>
> Sincerely,
> Emily

1. Did Emily's writing fit the purpose? Why or why not?

____

____

2. What should Emily have said in her letter? Write one or two sentences.

____

____

B. Pretend you are writing about your favorite restaurant. For each purpose, write a strong idea.

1. Purpose: to describe something at the restaurant

   My Idea: ____

2. Purpose: to tell a funny story about the restaurant

   My Idea: ____

**Your audience is who will read your writing.
Make sure your idea fits your audience.**

A. Imagine you are going to write about a neighborhood carnival.
Who is the best audience for each idea below? Draw a line to
connect each idea to the correct type of writing.

Idea

1. a list of businesses that donated
   supplies to the carnival

2. why your friend should come
   with you

3. your secret fear of falling
   off the Ferris wheel

What to Write

a. a letter to a friend

b. a journal entry that only you
   will read

c. a news article for a local
   newspaper

B. Read this news article. Fix the words that need a capital letter.
Then follow the directions below.

Officer Saves Boy and Dog

Officer Sarah Goldman made a brave rescue last Sunday
night. Josh Hogan of Rose Valley was walking his dog by the
Pitt river when it began to rain very hard. The boy and his dog
were quickly swept into the rising river. Officer goldman was on
her way home when she saw Josh struggling to stay afloat. She
jumped into the river and carried the boy and his dog to safety.
The mayor called officer Goldman a hero.

Imagine you are Josh. You are going to write some letters about
what happened. Tell what you would write about in each one.

1. To: Officer Goldman

   Idea: ____

2. To: your best friend

   Idea: ____

Choose a strong idea.
A strong idea fits your purpose and audience.

A. Think of events that have happened at school. What ideas can you write about? Write them in the web.

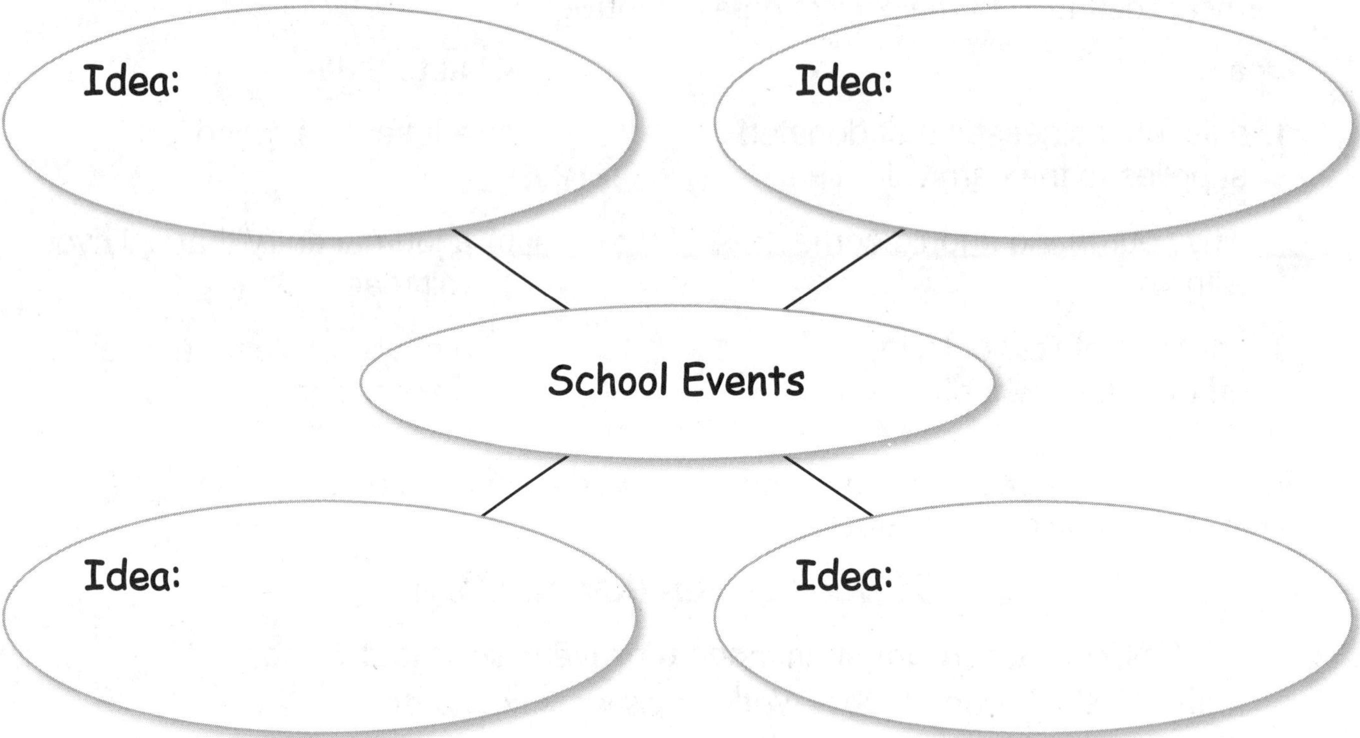

B. Pretend you are a reporter for the local newspaper. You will write a newspaper article about a school event. Answer the questions below.

1. What is the purpose of the article?

   ____

2. Who is your audience?

   ____

3. Which of your ideas in Activity A best fits the purpose and audience?
   Make a checkmark next to it.

Ideas

Write a news article about an event at your school. Include a headline.
Be sure to capitalize the names of people and places.

Headline: ____

____

____

____

____

____

____

____

____

____

____

____

____

____

____

____

____

____

Each paragraph should have a topic sentence so the reader understands what the paragraph is about.

A. Read this paragraph about a dog. Underline the topic sentence.

> Sammy was the best dog in the neighborhood. When her owners wanted to play, she played. When her owners were sad, Sammy made them feel better. She liked to visit everyone on her street. All her neighbors were glad to see her.

B. Read both paragraphs about people. Fix the sentences that do not have end marks. Then write an *X* next to the paragraph that does not have a topic sentence. Underline the topic sentence in the other paragraph.

☐ First, Chris moved to Water Street. Then, he lived on Baker Hill. After that, he moved across town to Knowles Ridge. Now, Chris is leaving for Bay Avenue

☐ Grandma Marie makes delicious cakes She knits blankets for us. What else can she do She likes to use her power drill, and she built our bookshelves. Grandma Marie can do many things!

C. Reread the paragraph you wrote an *X* next to in Activity B. Write a topic sentence for it.

Topic Sentence: ____

____

Ideas Each paragraph should have a topic sentence with good supporting details.

A. Read each persuasive paragraph. Which paragraph has details that support its underlined topic sentence? Write an *X* next to it. Then fix the sentences in both paragraphs that do not have correct end marks.

☐ <u>When you vote for student council, vote for Elizabeth!</u> She helped put on the ice-cream party last year. She asked us what kind of field trips we wanted? Then she talked to the principal. He listened to her, and we got to visit the Space Museum! Elizabeth can help us have a good year.

☐ <u>When you vote for student council, vote for Daniel.</u> He has a new bike. He has a lizard named Jinks. I go to his house on Saturdays. He is on my basketball team. We carpool to the games because he lives down the street. His dad knows my dad. And do you know what. Daniel's birthday is in March.

B. Imagine that your city or county has an award for the best school. What details would you use to persuade the judges that your school is the best in town? Write as many as you can think of below.

____

____

____

____

____

____

Ideas — Each paragraph should have a topic sentence with good supporting details.

A. Read each group of sentences. Write *TS* next to the topic sentence.
Write *D* next to each supporting detail.

1. _____ He travels in an envelope.

   _____ Stanley can fit into small spaces.

   _____ Stanley wakes up flat one day.

   _____ He has been crushed by a bulletin board!

   _____ Flat Stanley is an unusual book.

2. _____ The pictures help you learn the words.

   _____ G is for Googol is a fun alphabet book about math words.

   _____ You can learn 26 new words.

   _____ There are many pictures in G is for Googol.

   _____ Did you know that a googol is a very large number?

B. Choose a group of sentences above. Write the sentences in
a paragraph. Make sure each sentence ends with the correct
end mark.

____

____

____

____

____

____

Ideas

Each paragraph should have a topic sentence with good supporting details.

Think of a favorite book you read last year. Plan a summary paragraph about it. Write a topic sentence about the book in the top box. Write supporting details in the other boxes.

My Favorite Book: ____

Topic Sentence:

Supporting Detail:

Supporting Detail:

Supporting Detail:

Supporting Detail:

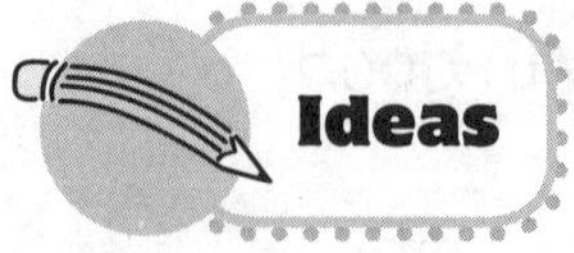

Write a summary paragraph about a favorite book. Remember to include a topic sentence with details that support it.

Be sure to use correct end marks.

Details tell what your main character is like.
They help the character seem like a real person.

Look at the pictures of the characters. Pretend you are writing
a story about each one. Answer the questions to add details.

1. What is the character's name?

   ____

2. What does he look like?

   ____

   ____

3. What does he like to do?

   ____

4. What would he say if his bike were stolen?

   ____

5. What is the character's name?

   ____

6. What does she look like?

   ____

   ____

7. What does she like to do?

   ____

8. What does she say when she looks in the mirror?

   ____

Ideas Choose the right setting for your story. A good setting helps your reader "see" where the action takes place.

A. Read the story ideas. Draw a line from each story idea to the setting that makes the most sense.

Story Idea

1. Spaceships battle for control of a planet.

2. Letter carriers ride horseback to deliver the mail.

3. A family takes an adventurous trip on a boat.

4. A sad dragon searches for its mother.

Setting

a. America's western states in the year 1850

b. an imaginary forest

c. the Amazon River today

d. outer space in the year 2500

B. Choose a story idea and a setting from Activity A. Imagine what the setting is like. Then answer the questions.

1. What can you see, hear, touch, taste, and smell in this place? Use adjectives to describe your answers.

____

____

____

____

2. What would a character say about this place? Finish the sentence. Use a comma and quotation marks in the dialogue.

_______________ says _______________________

____

The plot is the order of events in a story. A plot has an introduction, a turning point, and a conclusion.

A. Read this story. Fill in commas and quotation marks where they are needed for dialogue.

Leo and the Bird

John and Brianna were at home, doing homework. Their cat, Leo, was fast asleep at John's feet.

All of a sudden, there was a bang! A bird had flown into the glass door and was lying motionless on the porch. In a flash, Leo woke up and darted across the room and through his cat door. "He's going to catch the bird! John yelled.

Brianna and John quickly opened the door and ran outside. But Leo already had the bird in his mouth!

If you hold him down, I'll try to rescue the bird Brianna told John. Together, the two of them pounced on Leo. Brianna gently pried the bird from his mouth. It was still alive!

Quickly, she ran to the front yard while John brought Leo inside and locked the cat door. The bird was still at first, but then it flew away. Brianna came back into the house and told John that the bird was OK. "Nice try, Leo she said. But don't try that again!"

B. Put these events in order. Write the letter of each sentence on its part of the plot diagram.

a. A bird crashes into the window.

b. Brianna tells Leo to never try that again.

c. John and Brianna are doing homework.

d. John and Brianna take the bird from Leo.

e. Leo catches the bird.

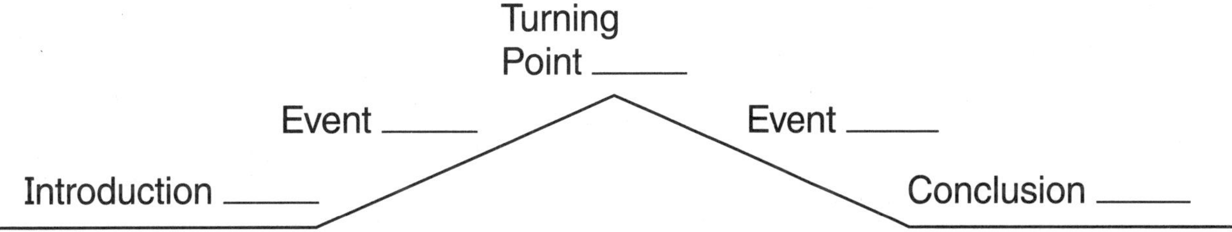

Ideas

To develop a good story, plan your characters, setting, and plot before you write.

Answer the questions to plan a story about someone who rescues an animal.

1. Who is the main character?

   ____

2. Describe your character.

   ____

   ____

   ____

3. Where and when is the setting?

   ____

   ____

4. List two things to describe in the setting.

   ____

   ____

5. Tell two things that happen in the story.

   ____

   ____

   ____

Write a story about someone who rescues an animal. Include dialogue in your story.

Be sure to use correct punctuation in the dialogue.

Ideas When you give information, write about the "5 Ws." Tell *who, what, when, where,* and *why.*

A. Read this report about an explorer. Underline the words or phrases that tell *who, what, when, where,* and *why.*

Ferdinand Magellan

Ferdinand Magellan was one of the greatest explorers in history. In 1519, he sailed from Spain to South America. He wanted to figure out how to get from the Atlantic Ocean to the Pacific Ocean. Ferdinand's expedition was the first one to cross the Pacific Ocean and return to Europe. He is known as the first explorer to sail around the world.

B. Read this biography of another explorer. Use the checklist to check whether the writer included the "5 Ws." Then answer the question.

Tenzing Norgay

Tenzing Norgay was born in a village. He was a very skilled mountain climber. Once, he rescued someone from a very high mountain. Tenzings mother knew he was very fit. She was right. Tenzing went on to become one of the first people to climb the world's highest mountain. He lived to be 72 years old.

> ### "5 Ws" Checklist
> ☐ Who ☐ What ☐ When ☐ Where ☐ Why

What details do you think the writer should add to the biography?

____

____

C. Reread the biography in Activity B. Find the possessive noun that needs an apostrophe. Add an apostrophe.

Don't just "tell" about your topic. Elaborate with examples that "show" what you mean.

A. Read each pair of sentences. Write an *S* next to the sentence that shows its topic. Write a *T* next to the sentence that just tells about it.

1. _____ Megan was angry.

   _____ Megan yelled, "Get out of my room!"

2. _____ The movie made me laugh so hard, I thought my jaw would fall off.

   _____ I liked the funny movie.

3. _____ The boys' uncle has to duck down just to walk in the front door of the house.

   _____ The boys' uncle is really tall.

B. Read this fantasy story. Fix the possessive noun that needs an apostrophe. Then underline three sentences that just "tell." Rewrite those sentences with details that "show."

Night Ride

Victoria went to bed. Then she fell asleep. The next thing she knew, a unicorn was in her bedroom. She hopped onto the unicorn's back, and it took her on a ride through a forest. She saw other unicorns. Victoria thought the whole thing was a dream. But when she woke up, she was holding a bunch of blue ribbons. They were ribbons she had seen before, tied to all of the unicorns horns.

____

____

____

____

Ask others to read your writing. They can help you find ideas and details to elaborate on.

A. Zack started writing a personal narrative about the first day of school. Read his draft. Fix the possessive nouns.

Crazy First Day

The first day of school was bad. Our neighborhoods power went out. Everyone got up late. Then our dog hopped out of the van. He followed a little girl into the girls bathroom. Then he jumped up on one of the teachers. He got the teacher's dress all dirty. I thought she was the other class' teacher. I was wrong. She was mine. I was in big trouble.

B. Zack needs to elaborate and add some details to his narrative. What should he tell more about? Write three questions you would ask Zack about his first day. Here are some phrases for starting your questions:

- Why did you…?
- Can you "show" how…?
- Why was there…?
- How did you feel when…?

1. ____

____

2. ____

____

3. ____

____

Ask others to read your writing. They can help you find ideas and details to elaborate on.

A. Think of a time when you gave a special gift to someone. What was the gift like? What happened when you gave the gift? Fill in the cluster with your ideas and details.

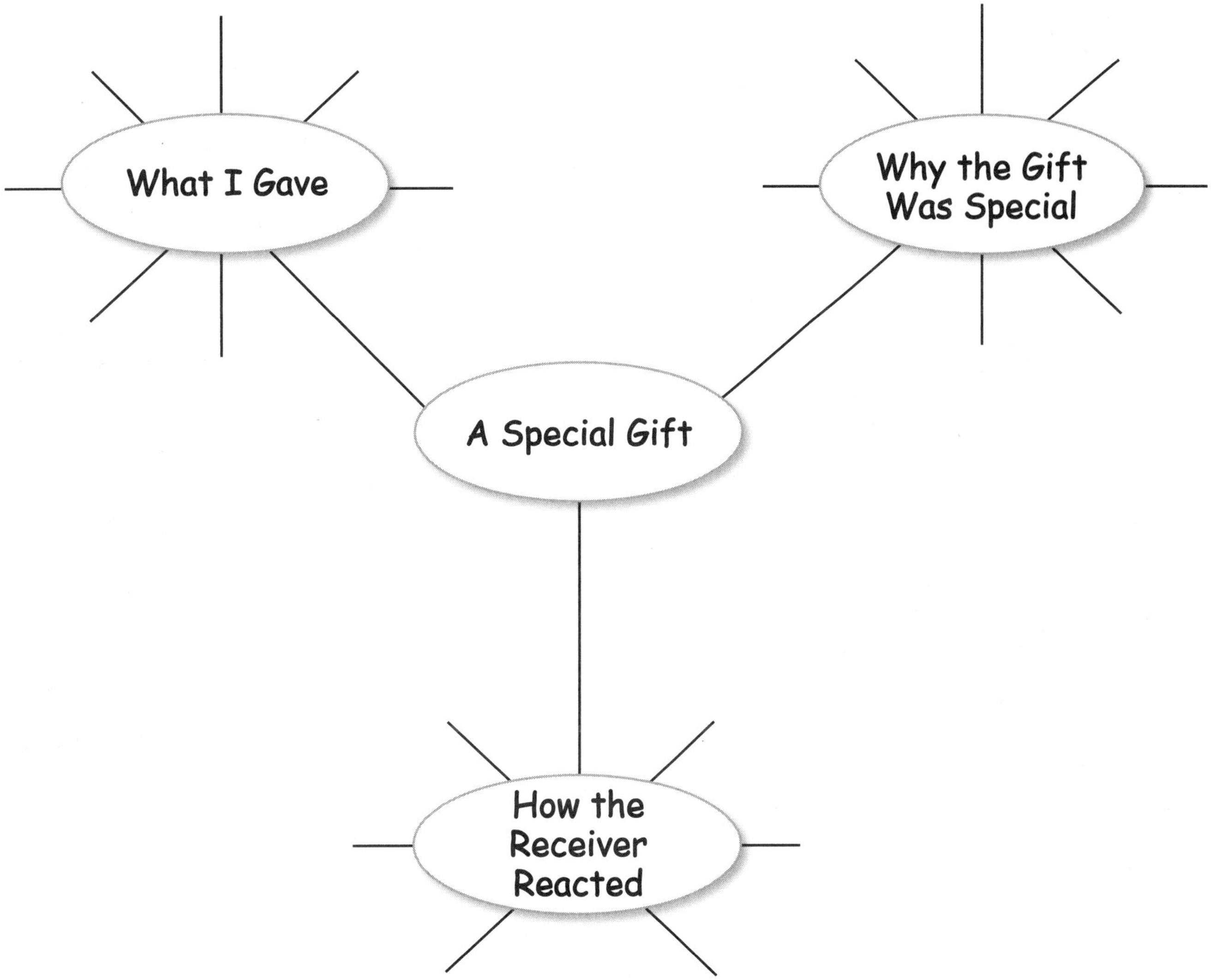

B. Share your cluster with a partner. Ask each other questions to help you think of what to elaborate on. Add the new details to your cluster.

Ideas

Write a personal narrative about giving a special gift to someone.
Be sure all of your possessive nouns have correct spelling and punctuation.

Ideas Stay focused on your topic when you write.

A. Read each television show review. Write an *X* next to the review that does not stay on topic. Delete the sentences that do not belong with the topic.

Gumby

☐ "Gumby" is a clay-animation cartoon about a little green man made of clay. Gumby changes his shape and twists himself in all kinds of ways. When he opens a book, he becomes part of the story. Once, he was reading a cowboy story, and he became a sheriff who saved the town from a bandit! Sometimes you can catch "Gumby" on TV, but I like to check out the DVDs from the Main street library. The theme song says, "You should see what Gumby can do today!"

Dictionary Diva

☐ There is a cool new cartoon about a superhero named Dictionary Diva. She has secret powers. She can fight evil by using big words! In one episode, she stops Dr. Two-Brains from stealing. Stealing is wrong. Once, my little brother tried to steal a pack of gum from the supermarket. My mom made him return it. It's important to learn lessons. He was sad, but I know he'll understand some day.

B. Read each detail. Circle the one that can be added to the "Dictionary Diva" review in Activity A.

I want to be a superhero for Halloween.

My brother is only three years old.

Dictionary Diva looks like a normal girl who lives with a normal family.

C. Reread the review of "Gumby" in Activity A. Find the name of a place that needs capitalization. Mark the letters that should be capitals.

Ideas Stay focused on your topic. Take out any unnecessary details.

A. Read this story. Find and cross out the details that are not important to the story. Then find and correct the proper nouns that should begin with capital letters.

Abby and the Rocket

The year was 1969. Abby sat in the car, excitedly brushing her hair. She and Girl scout troop 883 were headed to Kennedy space Center to watch a rocket launch! If everything went right, she and her troop members would see a historical moment. History was an OK subject at school. Math was better. Today's space mission would be the first time that an astronaut set foot on the moon.

"I hope we don't miss it!" Abby's dad said, pointing to the stopped cars around them. Traffic was a nightmare! At least Abby's favorite song was on the radio. She hummed along to pass the time. She could never remember the name of the band that played it.

Time went on. The car had barely moved. Finally, Abby saw something moving out of the corner of her eye. It was the rocket in the sky! It had successfully lifted off. "Maybe some day I can be an astronaut," Abby thought. She ate a candy bar after that. She put the empty wrapper in her purse.

B. Write one detail the writer could add to the story.

____

____

____

____

Stay focused on your topic. Select important details before you write.

A. Rachel completed this sensory details chart so she could write a description of the Downtown Farmers' Market. Read the details in the chart. Then cross out any details you think are unnecessary.

See	• bright and shiny fruits and vegetables • stop sign
Hear	• the ross elementary school choir singing • a seller shouting, "Ripe tomatoes here!"
Smell	• sweet kettle corn
Taste	• spicy apple cider • gum I bought at a store earlier
Touch	• people bumping into you in the crowd • cold snow cones

B. Use the remaining details in Activity A to write a paragraph that describes the Downtown Farmers' Market. Be sure to capitalize all proper nouns.

____

____

____

____

____

____

____

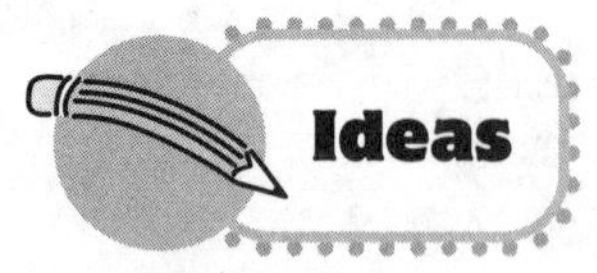

Ideas   Stay focused on your topic.

Think of a favorite place in your neighborhood or local area. Fill in the sensory chart with details that describe the place. Check to make sure your details are important and stick to your topic.

My Favorite Place: _______________________________

See	
Hear	
Smell	
Taste	
Touch	

Write a paragraph that describes a favorite place. Use sensory details from the chart you completed on Day 4.

Be sure to capitalize all proper nouns.

Organization — When you tell about events in a sequence, use transition words to signal when things happen.

A. Read this description of an event. Underline the transition words and phrases.

On March 2, Sunnyside Beach changed forever. During the past few days, storms had pounded the town. Giant waves had crashed over the fishing pier. A few days before, the Beach Patrol had closed the pier for safety. Then, on March 1, the pier began making creaking noises. At first, nobody cared. But as the day went on, the creaking became louder. Finally, everyone knew that the pier was falling down! The next day, people gathered on the beach to say goodbye to the pier. Meanwhile, the mayor and the city council were already planning to build a new, stronger pier.

B. Read this journal entry. Use the transition words in the box to complete the entry. Then find and correct the verbs that are in the wrong tense.

Transition Words		
as soon as	later	when
suddenly	today	

October 9, 2008

_______________, I saw Ms. Romero! _______________ we walk into the mall, I hear jazz music. _______________, I heard a familiar voice. _______________ I saw the singer, I thought it was Ms. Romero. Dad said it couldn't be her. We moved closer to get a better look. It <u>was</u> Ms. Romero, the principal of our school! _______________, I call Olivia and tell her what happened.

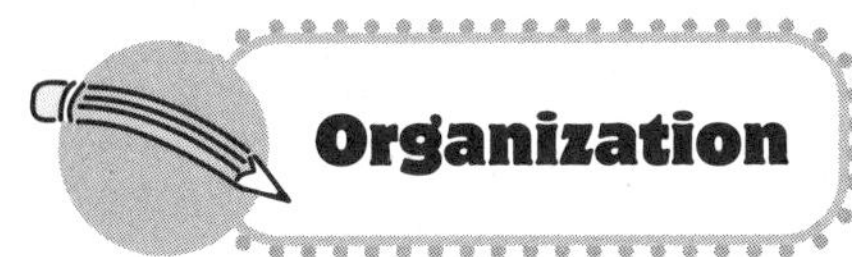

When you tell about a process, describe the steps in the correct sequence. Use transition words to signal the order.

A. The sequence map below shows how plastic bottles can be recycled into clothing. Read each sentence. Number the sentences in the correct sequence.

Recycling Plastic

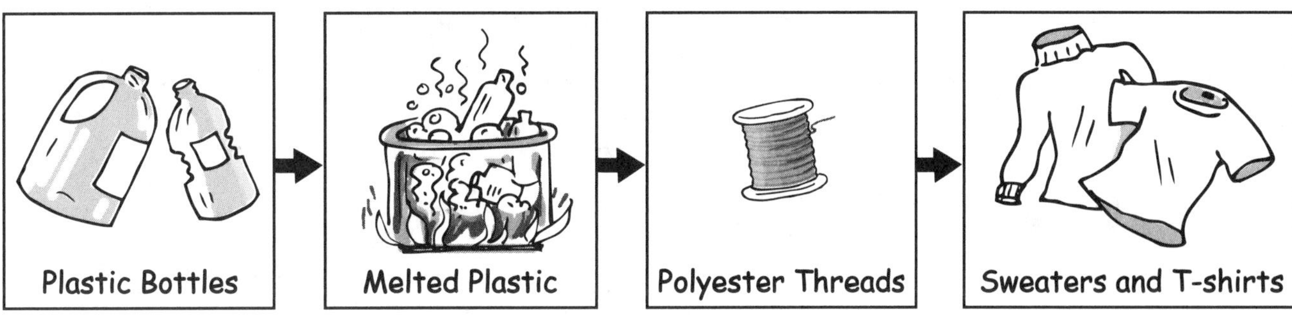

_____ The melted plastic is turned into polyester fibers.

_____ Plastic bottles are melted.

_____ The cloth is cut and sewn into sweaters and T-shirts.

_____ The polyester fibers are woven into cloth.

B. Write a paragraph about the recycling process. Use the numbered steps in Activity A and the transition words in the box. Make sure all of your verbs are in the correct tense.

Transition Words		
after	finally	first
next	then	

____

____

____

____

____

____

 **Organization**

In an autobiography, the events of someone's life should be in the order in which they happened.

A. Read Tony's autobiography. Fix the verbs that are in the wrong tense. Then answer the question.

> I was born at UCLA Medical Center in Los Angeles. When I was five years old, my sister Rachel teaches me how to read. I liked her comic books and I want to read them. But before that, my aunt, uncle, and cousin came to visit from Taiwan. We went to Disneyland. I was two years old, so I don't remember very much. Then, when I was seven years old, I join a soccer team. I've been playing soccer every year since. Finally, when I was eight years old, Rachel and I make our own comic book. It was called <u>Super Penguin</u>.

Which events are out of order? ___________________________________

____

B. Help Tony organize his life events in the correct sequence. Write what happened at each age in the correct order on the timeline.

Born: ____

Age: _____ _____________________________________

Age: _____ _____________________________________

Age: _____ _____________________________________

Age: _____ _____________________________________

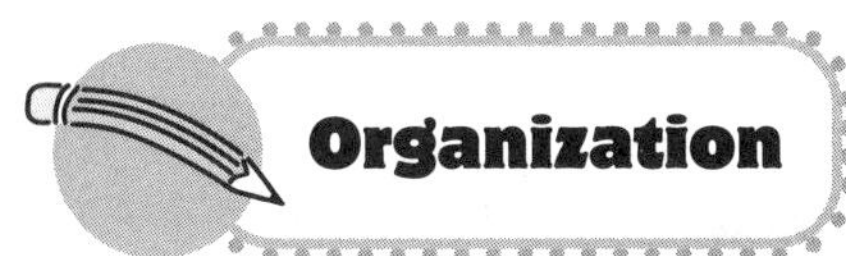

When you write your autobiography, put the events of your life in the correct sequence.

A. What important events would you include in your autobiography? Write them on the lines. For each one, write the year or how old you were.

Life Event: Year or Age:

B. Use the timeline to put your events in the correct sequence. Plot your events in the order in which they happened.

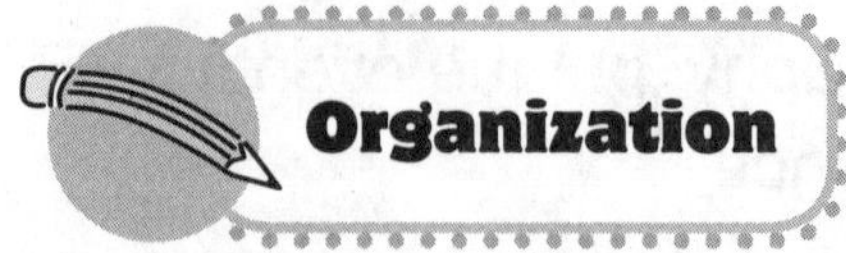

Write a short autobiography. Tell about events in your life in the order they happened.

Be sure all of your verbs are in the past tense.

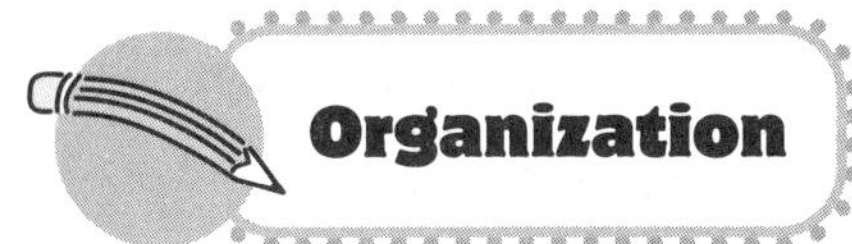

Organization   Use logical order in your paragraphs. Group similar details and connect them with transitions.

A. Paragraphs A and B were both written for a research report about animal groups, but they are organized differently. Read the paragraphs.

Paragraph A

All animals are part of an animal group. Frogs start as tadpoles in the water, and then they grow legs to live on land. A mammal drinks milk from its' mother. Owls and chickens are birds. All birds have feathers, but not all birds can fly. A bat is a mammal. Amphibians begin their life in the water, but they mostly live the rest of it on land. Dogs, whales, and humans are mammals. One group is birds. Bats are the only mammals that can fly! One group is amphibians.

Paragraph B

All animals are part of an animal group. One group is mammals. A mammal drinks milk from it's mother. Dogs, whales, and humans are mammals. A bat is also a mammal. In fact, bats are the only mammals that can fly! Another group is birds. All birds have feathers, but not all birds can fly. Owls and chickens are birds. Amphibians are one other group. They begin their lives in the water, but they mostly live the rest of it on land. For example, frogs start as tadpoles in the water, and then they grow legs to live on land.

1. Which paragraph was easier to understand? Why?

____

____

2. Find the word *its* and fix it if it is misspelled.

B. Reread Paragraph B. Circle each transition word or phrase.

Organization

Use logical order in your paragraphs. Group similar details and connect them with transition words.

A. Read the sentences. Write the two topics that the sentences tell about. Then number the sentences so they are in logical order.

_____ Hannah's family makes maple syrup from the maple trees on their farm.

_____ Vermont is known for delicious maple syrup.

_____ Its plain to see that Hannah is a true Vermont native!

_____ Hannah Teter is an Olympic snowboarder.

_____ Vermont is known for mountains and a long, snowy winter.

_____ Hannah grew up in Belmont, Vermont.

Topic 1: _______________________________

Topic 2: _______________________________

B. Use the sentences from Activity A to write a paragraph. Write your sentences in the order you numbered them. Use transition words to connect your sentences. Correct any errors you find in the word *its*.

Transition Words		
also	in fact	so

____

____

____

____

____

____

____

____

____

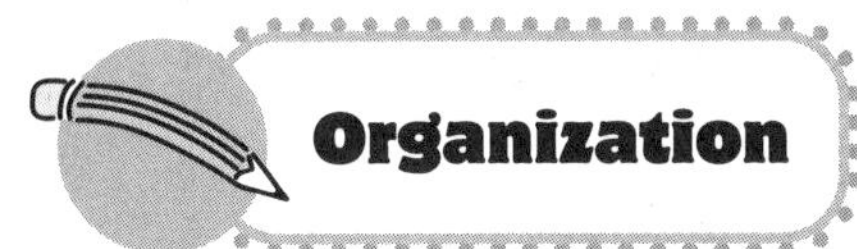

Organization   Use a graphic organizer to group similar details and to plan the order of your sentences.

A. Read each paragraph about a problem at school. Which paragraph is harder to follow? Write an *X* next to it.

☐ Sandals are very popular, but they don't protect your feet. Some kids are getting hurt on the playground when they run into something or try to kick a ball. We could make a rule against sandals. Then no one would get hurt. Some kids wouldn't like that because it's nice to wear sandals when it's hot. But I'd rather wear my sandals after school and on the weekends, just to be safe.

☐ A guard should hold up a large sign to warn drivers to stop. But our school doesn't have the money for a crossing guard. And drivers don't stop for students crossing the street. Crossing the street really is a big problem for our school. I think safety is more important. We may have to cut our cheerleading program to pay for a new crossing guard. A crossing guard would help.

B. Reread the paragraph you wrote an *X* next to in Activity A. Use the problem-and-solution diagram to reorganize the details in the correct order.

Problem (Tell what is wrong.)

Solution (Tell how the problem could be solved.)

Pros (Tell what is good about the solution.)	**Cons** (Tell about other problems the solution might cause.)

Use a graphic organizer to group similar details and to plan the order of your sentences.

Think of a problem in your school or community. How would you solve it? Use the problem-and-solution diagram to organize your ideas.

Problem: (Tell what is wrong.)

Solution: (Tell how the problem could be solved.)

Pros: (Tell what is good about the solution.)

Cons: (Tell about other problems the solution might cause.)

Write a problem-and-solution paragraph about a problem in your school or community and how you would solve it.

Be sure to spell *its* and *it's* correctly.

Organization — Organize your details by position. Describe a place by starting at one end and finishing at the other.

A. Read this description of a setting for a folk tale. Find the word *there* and fix it if it is misspelled. Then draw the setting in the box.

> Their were a lot of houses in a village. Some rows of crops were dry. A mountain was there. Large fields grew every kind of food the people could ever want. The river flowed. They're were only a few houses in another village. The two villages were the Village of Sorrow and the Village of Happiness.

B. Read another description of the setting. Draw it in the box. Then answer the question.

> The Village of Sorrow had only a few houses. Not many rows of crops grew there, and they were usually dry. Next to this village was the Great Mountain, which had a river running down its other side. The river flowed past the Village of Happiness, where there were many houses. Large fields grew every kind of food the people could ever want.

Which description was easier to visualize and draw? Why?

____

____

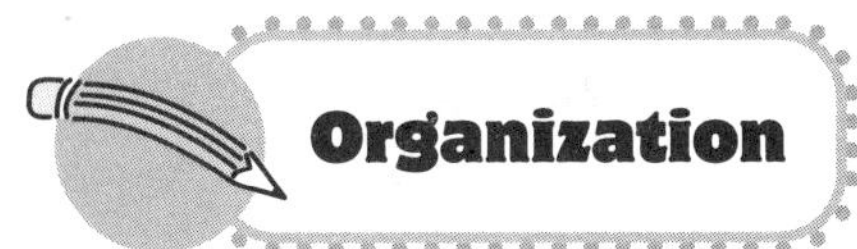

Organization — Organize your details by position. Describe something by starting at one end and finishing at the other.

A. Look at the diagram of the leg bones. Finish the paragraph by describing the bones in the order of their positions from top to bottom. Use position words and phrases in your sentences.

Position Words
above
behind
below
between
in back of
in front of
top
under

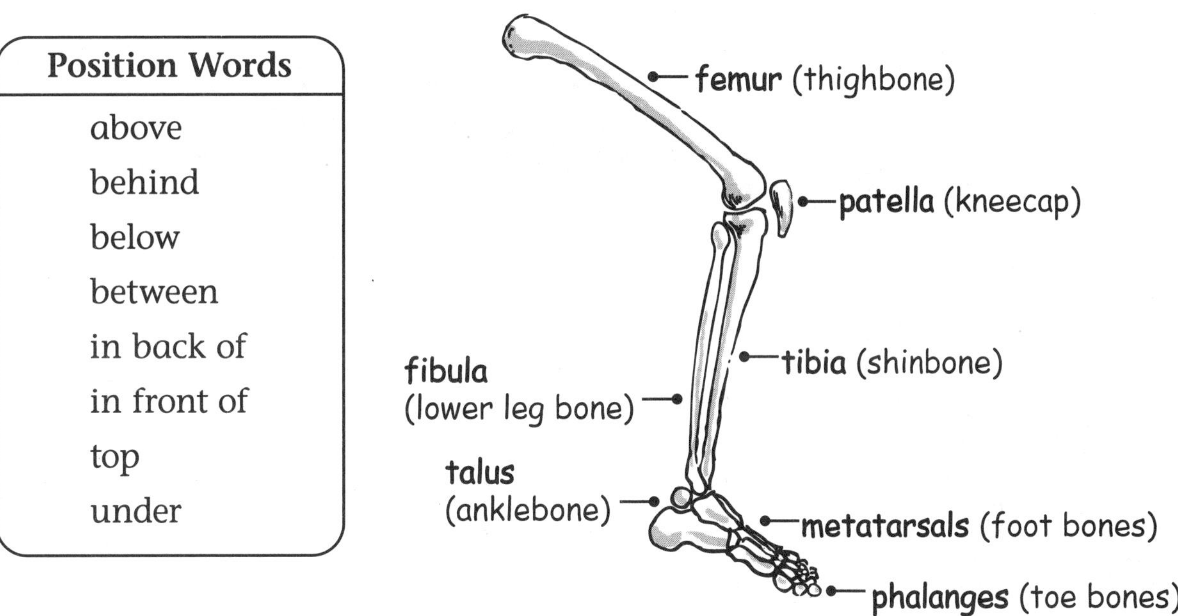

There are many leg bones. Their arranged in this order:
The femur is the top leg bone. ______________________________

____

____

____

____

____

B. Reread the first three sentences in the paragraph above. Correct the misspelled word using proofreading marks.

Organization   Look at a picture or diagram to help you organize your details by position.

Look at the front of the postcard. Then write a paragraph describing the amusement park. Organize your details by position, and use position words and phrases.

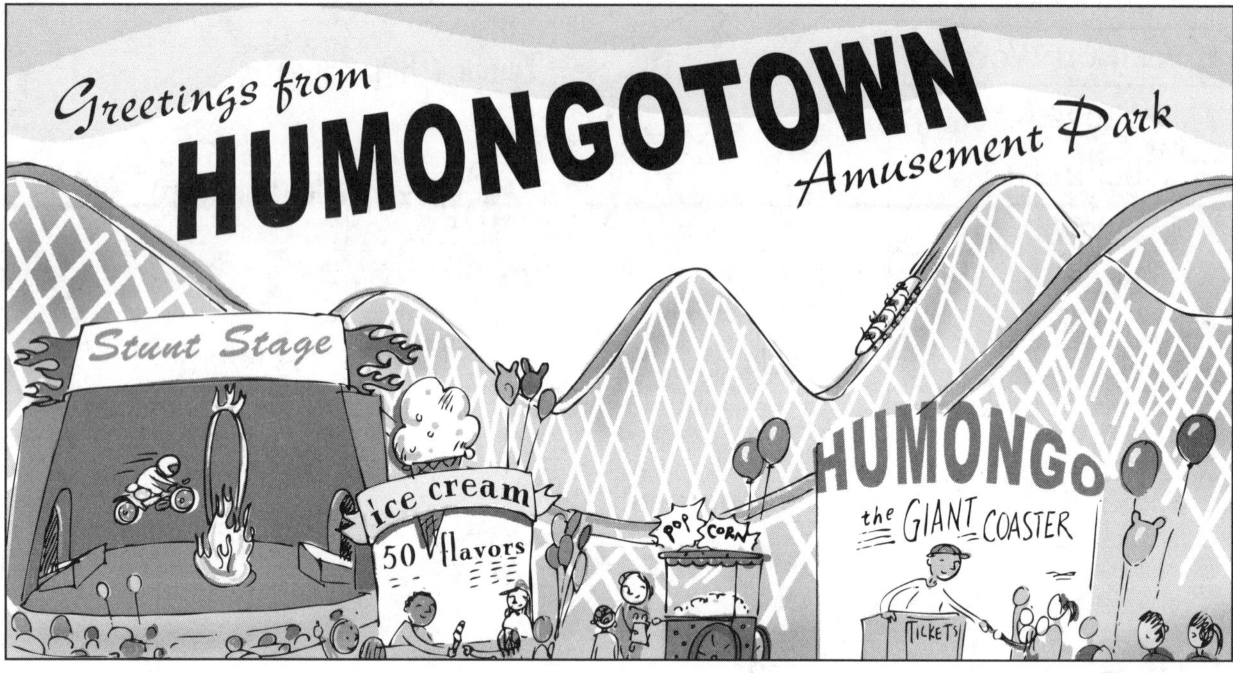

Dear Jennifer,

____

____

____

____

____

____

Your friend,

____

POSTAGE

UNITED STATES

Jennifer Olio

621 Pebble St.

Cold Junction, CA

92633

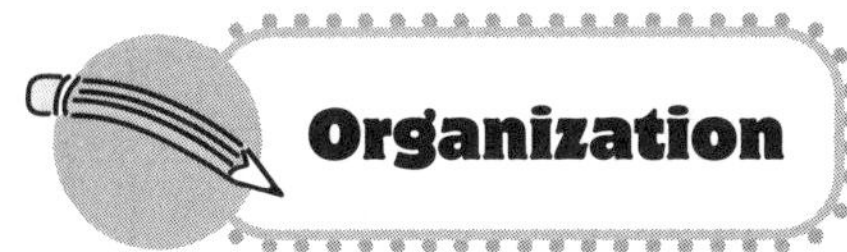

Draw a picture to plan your writing. A picture helps you organize your details by position.

A. Think of a place you've been to. Draw a postcard of it in the frame below. Label and draw lines to different parts of the picture on your postcard.

B. Write at least four position words and phrases you can use to tell about different parts of your picture.

_______________________________   _______________________________

_______________________________   _______________________________

_______________________________   _______________________________

Organization

Write a postcard describing a place where you've been. Describe the place you drew on Day 4, going from one end of the picture to the other. Use describing and position words in your sentences.

Be sure to spell *their, there,* and *they're* correctly.

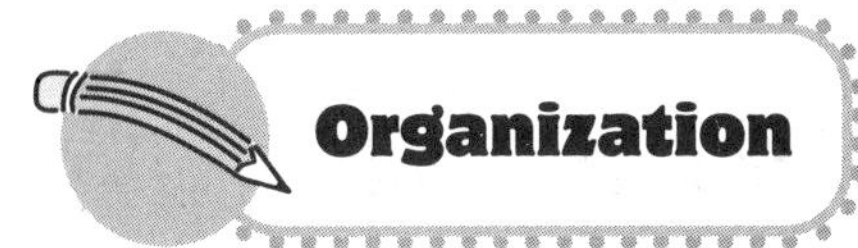

Organize your paragraph by telling how two things are alike. Then tell how they are different.

A. Read this book report about two books. Draw a straight line under the sentences that tell how they are alike. Draw a wavy line under the sentences that tell how they are different.

The Invention of Hugo Cabret and Harry Potter and the Sorcerer's Stone are books about young boys. Both boys' parents have died. Hugo is sent to live with his uncle. Harry is sent to live with his uncle and his aunt, too. However, The Invention of Hugo Cabret takes place in Paris, France, about a hundred years ago. Harry Potter and the Sorcerer's Stone takes place in England and Scotland, in modern times. Although Harry has special powers, Hugo does not. Still, Hugo is a genius at fixing clocks and toys.

B. Read this paragraph from a research report. Use the words in the boxes to complete the paragraph. Then find and fix the incorrect verbs.

Alike	
both	similarly

Different		
although	but	on the other hand

_______________ Scotland and France are countries in Europe. Scotland is home to Edinburgh Castle, which are more than a thousand years old! _______________, France has a very famous castle called Chambord. _______________ the two countries is close, they speak different languages. English is the main language of Scotland, _______________ French are the main language of France. Scotland still has a monarch—Queen Elizabeth II. _______________, France no longer has a king or queen.

Organize your paragraph by telling how two things are alike or different, one point at a time.

A. Read the paragraph about two games. Find and fix the incorrect verbs. Then answer the questions.

> [1] Two great ballgames is tetherball and tennis. [2] In tetherball, players hit a ball that are tied to a pole. [3] In tennis, players use a racket to hit a ball over a net. [4] A tetherball court are a small circle where two people stand. [5] On the other hand, a tennis court are a large rectangle, where up to four people can run around. [6] In tetherball, players try to hit the ball so the other player can't hit it back. [7] Likewise, in tennis, players try to do the same thing.

1. What are both sentences 2 and 3 about?

____

2. What are both sentences 4 and 5 about?

____

3. What are both sentences 6 and 7 about?

____

B. Read each sentence. Draw a line to the sentence it should appear next to in a paragraph.

The Plasto-Bricks Building Set

1. You can build unlimited kinds of buildings to play in.

2. It comes with 4 character action figures.

3. You can play with whomever you are with.

The Brick Tower Video Game

a. You can play only in the Tower.

b. You can play with friends or neighbors over the Internet.

c. You can choose from 8 characters.

A Venn diagram can help you see how things are alike and different so you can plan your writing.

A. Read the chart. Use the information about Sydney and James to fill in the Venn diagram.

	Sydney	James
Birthday Month	July	July
Favorite Sport	soccer	basketball
School	San Antonio School	San Antonio School
Teacher	Mr. Zaccaro	Ms. Rocklin

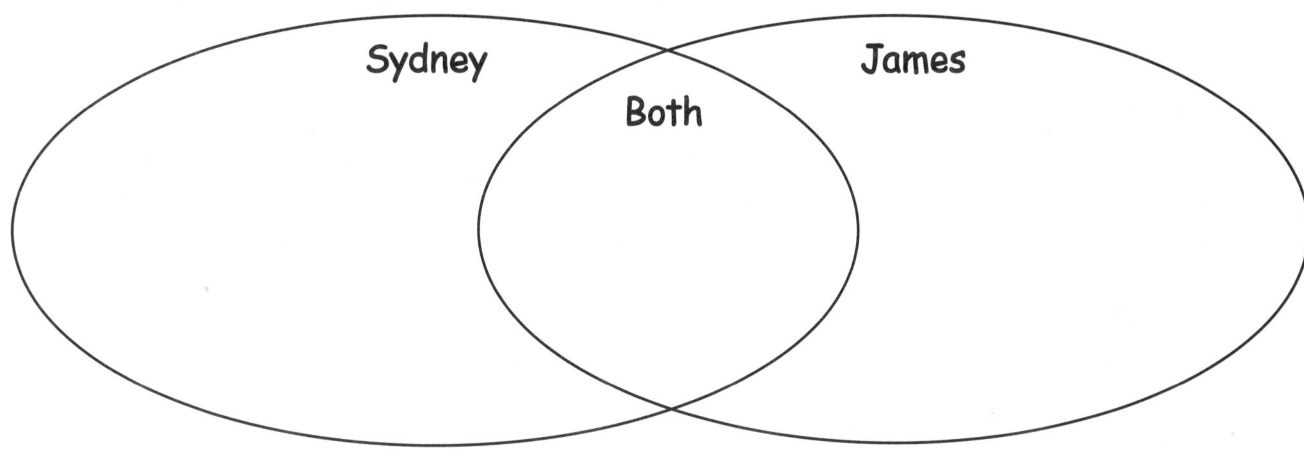

Transition Words

also   both   but   however   similarly   on the other hand

B. Write a paragraph that tells how Sydney and James are alike and different. Use transition words.

____

____

____

____

____

Organization Use a Venn diagram to plan your writing about how two things are alike or different.

A. Use the questions on the left side of the chart to interview two people. Write their answers in the blank spaces.

Questions	Name:	Name:
1. Where do you go to school?		
2. What is your favorite color?		
3. Do you have a pet? If so, what kind?		
4. What is your favorite subject?		
5. What is your least favorite sport?		

B. Use your answers from Activity A to fill in the Venn diagram.

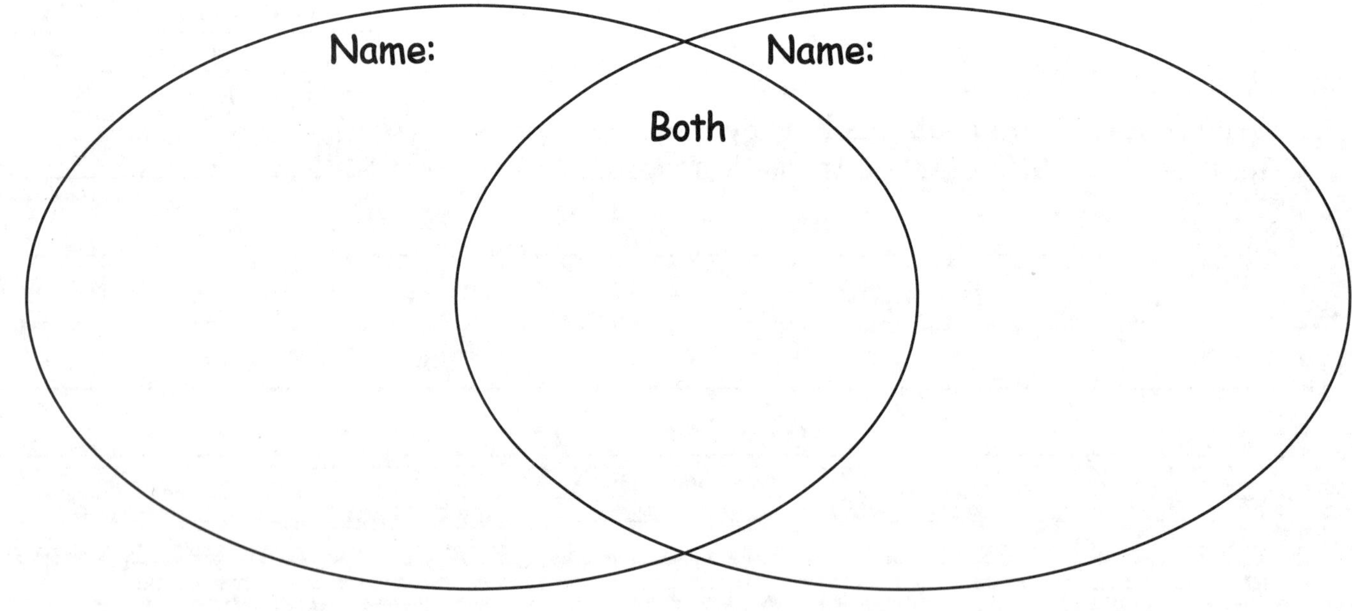

Organization

Write a paragraph that tells how two of your classmates are alike and different. Include transition words to help guide and organize your ideas.

Be sure to use *is* and *are* correctly.

Organization

The best way to organize your writing depends on your topic and purpose.

Decide which type of organization each paragraph uses. Write the correct letter on the line. Then fill in the missing parts of the organizers.

Paragraph

How It Is Organized

1. _____ Stevie Wonder was born in 1950. As a blind boy, he learned the harmonica, piano, and drums. He made his first album at age twelve! In the 1960s, 70s, and 80s, he had many hit songs. In 1999, he was honored by President Bill Clinton. Read more in Little Stevie Wonder by Quincy Troupe.

a. Problem-and-Solution:

Problem:

Solution: get businesses to help

Pro: will have money   **Con:** hard to find

2. _____ Students want to learn how to play music, but instruments cost too much. We could ask businesses to sponsor us. The businesses would pay for our instruments, and we would advertise the businesses at our concerts. It might be hard to find sponsors, but it's worth a try.

b. Position Order:

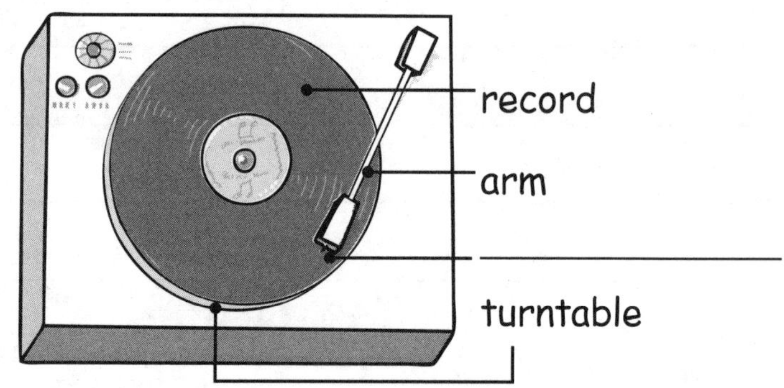

3. _____ Long before CDs and MP3s, music was played on a record player. It had a spinning plate called a turntable. Next to that was a pickup arm. At the end of the arm was a needle called a stylus. The turntable spun the record around, while the stylus read sound vibrations from grooves in the record.

c. Time Order:

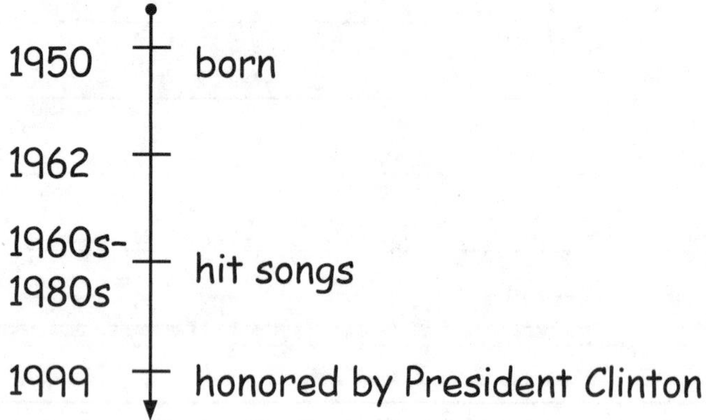

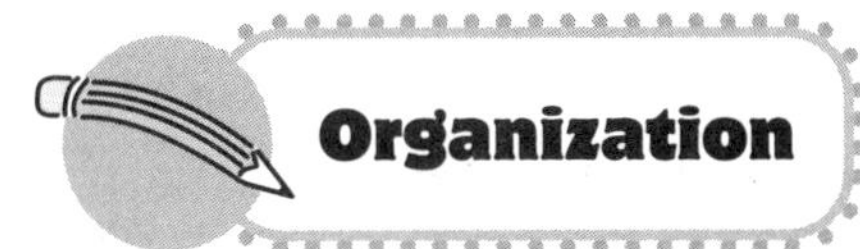

When you are given a writing assignment, decide what type of organization best fits the assignment.

A. Read each paragraph topic. Which type of organization would you use to write the paragraph? Write it on the line. Circle words in the description that give clues to your answer.

Types of Organization: Alike and Different, Position Order, Logical Order

Topic 1: Describe an ant colony, including what is in each part of the colony and how it is built.

____

Topic 2: Compare bees and ants, explaining how they are the same and different.

____

Topic 3: Tell how bees help humans, describing products made by bees and how they are made.

____

B. Read each transition word or phrase. Which kind of order is it usually used with? Write it in the correct column.

Transition Words		
also	between	in back of
another	both	in fact
below	however	so

Alike and Different	Position Order	Logical Order

Organization When you are given a writing assignment, first decide what type of organization fits the assignment.

A. Read Jose's writing assignment. Then look at each graphic organizer. Circle the organizer that Jose should use for organizing his paragraph.

Writing Assignment: Write a paragraph that tells how two movies are alike. Then tell how they are different. Give examples from each movie.

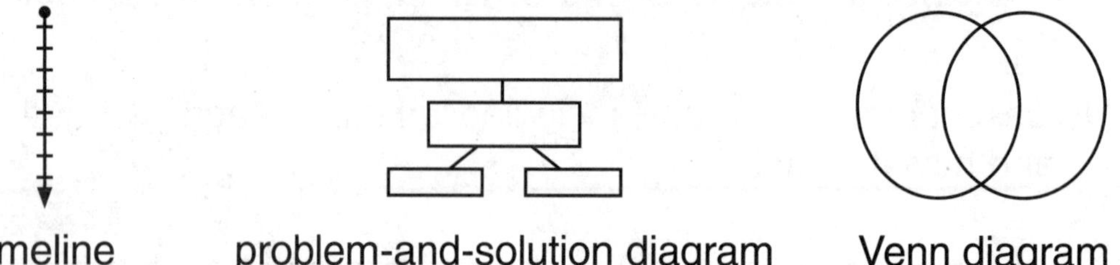

B. Read the sentences below. Underline the titles of movies. Then draw the graphic organizer you circled in Activity A. Write each sentence's number where it belongs in the organizer.

1. Mrs. Doubtfire and Mary Poppins are two movies about nannies.

2. Mary has magical powers, such as being able to fly.

3. The nanny in Mrs. Doubtfire is not magical, but he can disguise himself very well.

4. Mrs. Doubtfire does not have any songs or singing in it.

5. Mary Poppins is a musical movie in which the characters sing songs.

6. In both movies, the nanny teaches the kids to have a lot of fun.

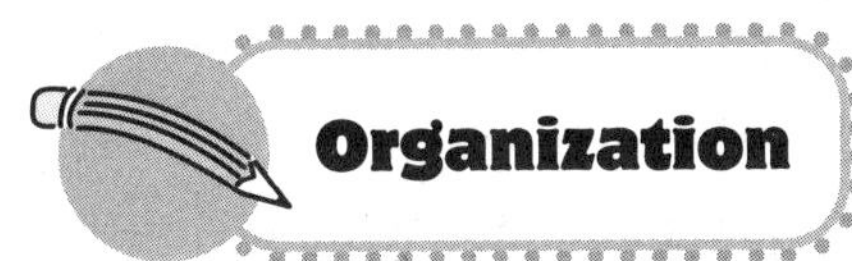

Organization When you are given a writing assignment, first decide what type of organization fits the assignment.

A. Read the writing assignment. Look at each graphic organizer. Circle the organizer that you would use for planning your paragraph.

Writing Assignment: Write a summary paragraph about a book you've read. Tell about the book's events in the order they happened.

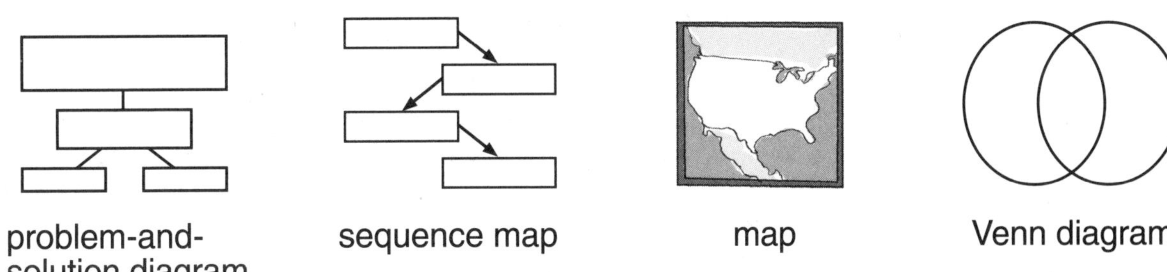

B. Copy the diagram you circled above and complete it about a book you've read.

Book Title: ____

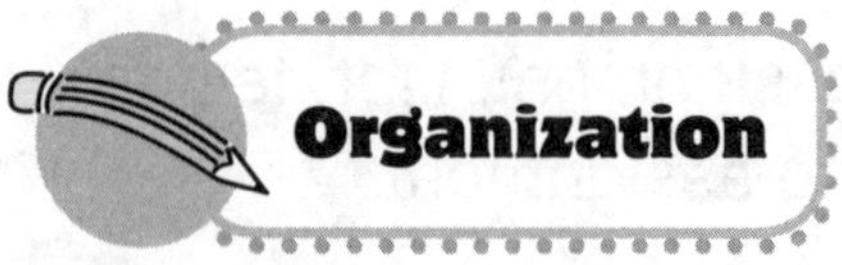

Organization

Write a summary paragraph about a book you've read. Tell about the book's events, using your sequence map from Day 4.

Remember to underline the title of the book you are writing about.

Choose vivid action verbs to tell your reader exactly what is happening. Avoid tired, overused verbs.

A. Read each poem. Pay special attention to the underlined words.

Poem A

Cousin Alexander
<u>Eats</u> our dinner,
<u>Makes us</u> play tag while
<u>Stepping on</u> the flowers,
<u>Breaks</u> all our toys, and
<u>Rests</u> while we <u>do</u> his dishes,
Before <u>going</u> back home.

At first, we <u>are happy</u>!
"He's gone!" we <u>say</u>. But then...
We <u>get</u> a little lonely.
And <u>then he's</u> here again.

Poem B

Cousin Alexander
<u>Gobbles up</u> our dinner,
<u>Forces us to</u> play tag while
<u>Trampling over</u> the flowers,
<u>Destroys</u> all our toys, and
<u>Snoozes</u> while we <u>scrub</u> his dishes,
Before <u>strutting</u> back home.

At first, we <u>rejoice</u>!
"He's gone!" we <u>cheer</u>. But then...
We <u>begin to feel</u> a little lonely.
And <u>we invite him</u> here again.

In which poem was the action easier to picture? Why?

____

____

B. Read each sentence. Fix any verbs that don't agree with their subjects. Then circle the tired verb. Replace it with a vivid verb and write the new sentence.

1. I goes up the hill.

____

2. Jasmine laugh at her brother's joke.

____

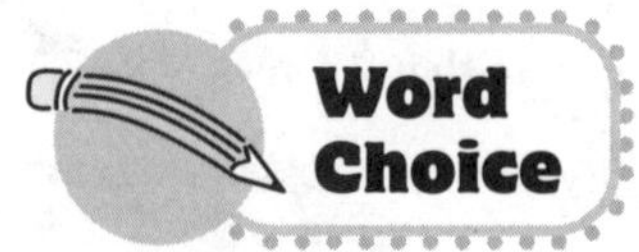

Learn the difference between similar action verbs. Choose the right one for your meaning.

A. Read each group of sentences. Fix the verbs that don't agree with their subjects. Then answer the questions.

1. The cat eat its tuna.

   The dog munches on its bone.

   The rabbit devours its carrot.

   Which animal sounds like it is eating the fastest? ________________________

2. Grace and Destiny race home after the game.

   Dylan and Anna trudge home after the game.

   Rob and Sam strolls home after the game.

   Who is probably the most tired after the game? ________________________

B. Read each pair of verbs. Both words have a similar meaning, but they are slightly different. Write an adverb for each word to make the meanings clearer.

1. step _________________   stomp _________________

2. weep _________________   wail _________________

3. mumble _________________   shout _________________

4. take _________________   grab _________________

5. soar _________________   fly _________________

Word Choice

Look for tired verbs in your writing. Change them to vivid action verbs.

Read this sequence paragraph. Use proofreading marks to fix three verbs that do not agree with their subjects. Then look for the tired verbs *get, put, go,* and *do.* Cross them out and replace them with vivid verbs from the box.

<table>
<tr><td colspan="4" align="center">Vivid Verbs</td></tr>
<tr><td>press</td><td>kneel</td><td>raise</td><td>spread</td></tr>
<tr><td>lift</td><td>return</td><td>practice</td><td></td></tr>
</table>

Down, Doggy, Down!

Yoga is excellent exercise for your mind and body. You can do yoga poses at home, once you learns them. Here are how to practice the "Downward Dog" pose: First, put your yoga mat on the floor. Get on the mat on your hands and knees. Make sure your hands are on the ground right under your shoulders, and your knees are directly under your hips. Keep your toes on the floor. Then, take a deep breath in. Next, breathe out while you put the palms of your hands on the floor. At the same time, put your hips up as high as possible. Straighten your legs as much as possible, and keep your back straight, too. Relax your head as you gently presses your heels down toward the floor. Take ten deep breaths. Finally, go to your starting pose, kneeling with your knees and hands on the mat.

Word Choice — Use vivid action verbs in your writing.

Think of a game or sport you like to play. Use the sequence map to write the steps for playing. For each step, use one or more vivid action words.

How to Play ____

Step 1:

↓

Step 2:

↓

Step 3:

↓

Step 4:

↓

Step 5:

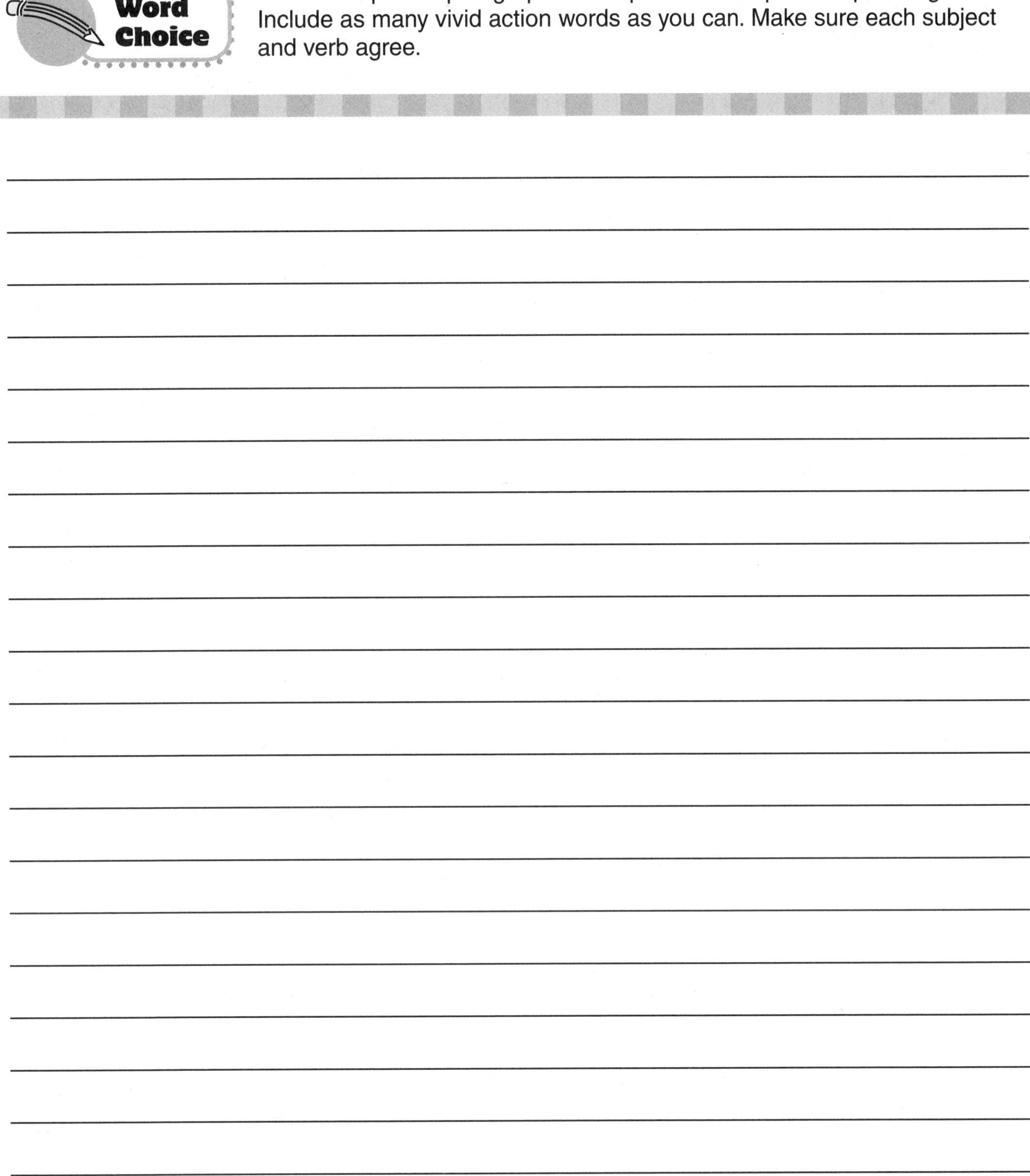

Word Choice

Write a sequence paragraph that explains the steps of a sport or game. Include as many vivid action words as you can. Make sure each subject and verb agree.

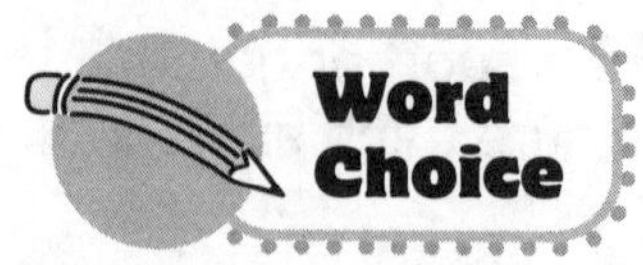

Sensory adjectives tell what something looks, sounds, smells, tastes, or feels like.

A. In each pair of synonyms, which word is just OK, and which one is better? Write each word in the correct column on the chart.

	Just OK	Better
1. fast • rhythmic	___________	___________
2. icy • cold	___________	___________
3. towering • big	___________	___________
4. good • fragrant	___________	___________
5. bitter • bad	___________	___________

B. Read this part of a story. Think of a better sensory word to replace each word in parentheses. Write the new word on the line.

Mrs. Russo was ______________ . Ben and Haley had asked her
(hungry)
to judge their pizza bake-off. She could smell the ______________
(tasty)
pepperoni. Finally, Ben and Haley came out of the kitchen, each

holding their own ______________ pizza. Mrs. Russo noticed the
(warm)
______________ , stringy cheese on Ben's pizza. On the other hand,
(hot)
Haley's sauce tasted very ______________ .
(good)

"Well?" Haley asked with an expectant impatient look.

"I'll need to finish both pizzas to decide!" Mrs. Russo declared.

C. Reread the story. Insert a comma where it is needed between two adjectives.

Word Choice

Use adjectives and adverbs to make your sentences more descriptive.

A. Look at the pictures of Kevin and Natalie. Then read each sentence. Rewrite the sentences, adding adjectives and adverbs. If necessary, use a comma between two adjectives.

1. Natalie reels in the fish.

____

2. Kevin reclines in the chair.

____

3. Natalie holds her little sister.

____

4. Kevin glides over the snow.

____

B. Picture yourself doing something you enjoy. Write a sentence that describes what you are doing. Use at least one adverb and two adjectives in your sentence.

____

____

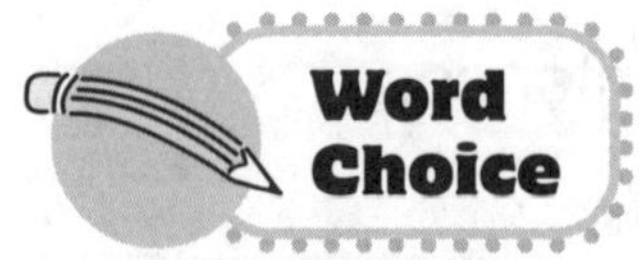

Word Choice

Use sensory adjectives and adverbs when you want your writing to be persuasive.

Read each toy advertisement. Write a sensory adjective or a strong adverb where it is needed. Make sure you put a comma between two adjectives.

Turf Rider Remote-Control Truck

This _______________ _______________ truck is
(adjective)   (adjective)

nonstop fun!

The thick wheels _______________ turn the truck
(adverb)

wherever you want to go.

The truck is _______________, so you can go up
(adjective)

steep hills.

Jump 'n' Joy Trampoline

Get exercise and have fun with this _______________
(adjective)

_______________ trampoline.
(adjective)

It's sturdy, so you can jump _______________.
(adverb)

Able to fit 3 people, this trampoline is _______________!
(adjective)

Word Choice

Use sensory adjectives and adverbs when you want to persuade.

Imagine you are writing an advertisement for an animal shelter. You want to persuade people to adopt the animals that live there. Write vivid adjectives about each animal. Write adverbs that describe the action words.

1. Dog _______________ _______________
   (adjective)   (adjective)

   plays _______________
   (adverb)

   learns tricks _______________
   (adverb)

2. Cat _______________ _______________
   (adjective)   (adjective)

   purrs _______________
   (adverb)

   snuggles _______________
   (adverb)

3. Guinea Pig _______________ _______________
   (adjective)   (adjective)

   squeaks _______________
   (adverb)

   plays _______________
   (adverb)

Write an advertisement for an animal shelter. Describe three animals that you want your readers to adopt. Use sensory adjectives and adverbs. Be sure to use commas between two or more adjectives in a row.

Word Choice A simile compares two things, using the words *like* or *as*. Similes make your writing unique.

A. Read each poem. Circle the word *like* or *as* in each one.
Underline the two things that are being compared.

1. Math
Piles of numbers
As high as the sky,
Word problems, division,
You name it, I'll try!

2. Skateboarding
Down the steep hill,
Wheels rolling like thunder,
"How will I stop?"
I panic and wonder.

3. Camping
The stars are all shining
Like tiny flashlights,
We set up our tents,
We say our good-nights.

B. Which of the poems did you like the best?
Write the title using quotation marks.

____

C. Read this sentence. Rewrite it as a simile, using *like* or *as*
to compare the underlined subject to something else.

<u>Ethan</u> runs fast!

____

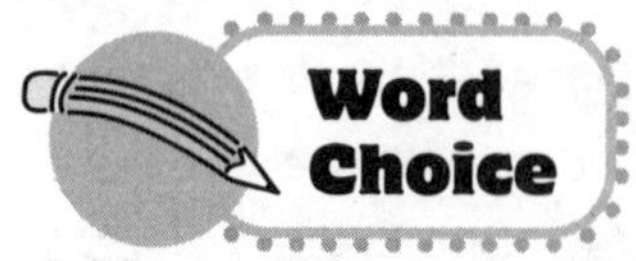

A metaphor compares two things, without using the words *like* or *as*.

A. Read this story. Then answer the questions.

Growing

Over a hundred years ago, a Chinese boy named Chong stowed away on a ship. The ship landed in San Francisco. Chong grew up and got married. He and his wife bought a house in San Francisco. They were setting down their roots. Soon, they had children. Then their children grew up and had families. The family tree grew bigger and bigger, with more branches growing off it. Chong's grandchildren had children. Some of the family moved to different parts of the country. Soon, the tree's branches were spread all over the land. But the roots of this mighty tree were still with Chong, in his little house in San Francisco.

1. What two things are being compared in the story? Write a complete sentence, including the title of the story. Use quotation marks.

   ____

2. Think about the two things that are being compared. How are they alike? List two ways.

   • ____

   • ____

B. Which one of these would be a better metaphor for a movie? Why?

   • a plane ticket to a new, exciting place

   • a big, comfortable chair

   ____

Use similes and metaphors to describe something.

Read this description of a song. Then answer the questions.

"Ba-Boom" of Doom

I hear it when I wake up in the morning. I hear it when I go to sleep. I hear it when I'm trying to think of an answer during a social studies test. It's the "Ba-Boom" song from the Wham Energy Drink commercial! The song starts out soft. "Ba-boom, ba-boom, here's a can for you," it says. Then it gets really loud, with a drumbeat that goes really fast. The worst part about it is that a lot of people like the song. The song follows me wherever I go! My little sister sings it in the car. The kids sing it at school. The bus driver sings it when we get on the bus. "Here's a can for you, and you, and you, and you," he says, as he points to each of us. The song really wears me out! I thought I could escape it in my sleep. But, when I close my eyes, guess what I hear? "Ba-boom, ba-boom..."

1. Write three similes to describe the song.

    • ____

    • ____

    • ____

2. What is a good metaphor for the song? What could you compare the song to? Give two reasons for your answer.

    Metaphor: ____

    Reason 1: ____

    Reason 2: ____

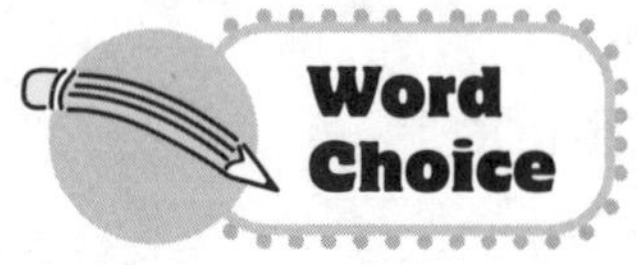

Use similes and metaphors to describe something.

Think of a song you like or dislike. Write the title of the song, using quotation marks. Then answer the questions.

Song Title: _______________________________

1. Write three describing words that tell about the song.

   _________________ _________________ _________________

2. How does the song make you feel?

   ____

   ____

   ____

   ____

3. What can you compare the song to?

   ____

   ____

   ____

What do the two have in common?

   • ____

   • ____

   • ____

   • ____

Word Choice

Describe a song you like or dislike. Use a simile or a metaphor to tell how the song makes you feel.

Write the title of the song in quotation marks.

Word Choice — Use informal language with friends and family. Use formal language when your reader could be anyone.

Stephanie wrote about her school food drive in her journal. She also wrote a news article about it for the school newsletter. Read both paragraphs. Then answer the questions.

Journal Entry

The weather was totally cold this morning. We got to the food drive at 7:00. Everyone's parents were dropping off cans and boxes and stuff. All of a sudden, we were like, "Whoa!" We saw a HUGE truck coming. It was packed with food from Asad's Market! We were all, "That's totally cool!" This food drive was super fun. Everyone did a good job!

News Article

On the morning of the food drive, the weather was very cold. Volunteers arrived as early as 7 a.m.! Throughout the morning, many parents brought cans and boxes of vegetables, meat, and rice. Suddenly, we were stunned to see a large truck backing up into the schoolyard. The truck was filled with food from Asad's Market. We thanked Mr. Asad for his thoughtful donation. Everyone decided the food drive went very good!

1. Which writing uses more formal language? _______________________
   Underline words or phrases that sound formal.

2. Which writing uses informal language? _______________________
   Underline words or phrases that sound informal.

Know the difference between formal and informal language.

A. Read each pair of words or phrases. Write *F* next to the one that is formal. Write *I* next to the one that is informal.

1. ask ___   request ___

2. How are you? ___ What's up? ___

3. lots of ___   many ___

4. stuff ___   items ___

5. awesome ___   wonderful ___

6. Goodbye ___   CUL8R ___

B. Read this formal letter. Find and correct the word that should be changed to *well*. Then rewrite the greeting and paragraph as if you were sending a friendly letter to someone you know.

Dear Mr. Enriquez,

    I am a member of the City Youth Orchestra. I play the trumpet. We are having our Winter Concert on January 10. Would you like to buy some tickets? They cost $10.00 for adults and $5.00 for children. I promise we will play very good. The money goes toward new instruments and classes. Please call me at 555-6024.

____

____

____

____

____

____

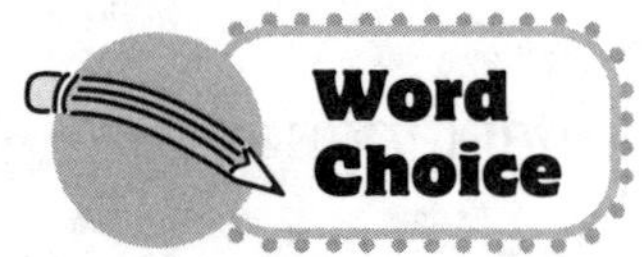

If you use polite, formal language when writing a letter, your reader will be more likely to listen to you.

Rebecca wrote a letter to a toy company to complain about a broken remote-control car she bought. Read the letter. Then rewrite it, using formal language. Fix the word that should be changed.

Hey Remote Possibilities Inc.,

The Crazee Car you sold me is a total dud. It doesn't work good at all. When I press "forward," the car goes backward. When I press "backward," the car goes forward! My BFF Brian says I should just hold the remote upside down and it will all make sense. LOL! At least I have a good sense of humor. But I'm returning your messed-up car anyway. Don't try to send me another one! Just give me my money back.

Thanks,
Rebecca Balboa

If you use polite, formal language when writing a letter, your reader will be more likely to listen to you.

Imagine your family went to a restaurant called Rusty's. This is what happened while you were there:

- It took an hour for the servers to bring your food.
- You ordered a burger, but they brought you liver and onions!
- Your mom's grilled chicken was cold.
- Your dad's ice-cream sundae was melted.

Plan a letter to the owner, Rusty McRussell, to complain about what happened. If you're nice and polite, he might give you your money back. Answer each question in a complete sentence, using formal, polite language.

1. Why are you writing this letter?

   ____

2. How was the food at Rusty's? Use three describing words.

   ____

   ____

3. How was the service at Rusty's? Use two describing words.

   ____

   ____

4. What do you want the owner to do?

   ____

   ____

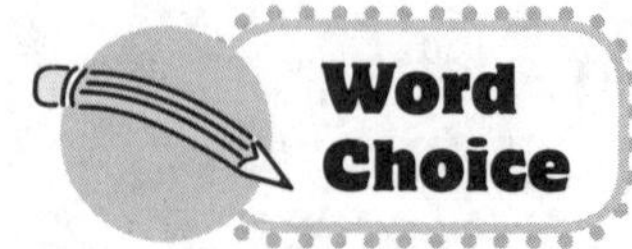

Word Choice

Write a letter to the owner of Rusty's Restaurant, telling him about your family's bad experience.

Use the words *good* and *well* at least once.

____
date

____

A good beginning gets the reader's attention.
One way to do this is to begin with a question.

A. Read each paragraph. Then answer the question.

Paragraph A

Do you enjoy watching movies? How about sunsets? If you like using your eyes, you'll love vitamin A! Vitamin A is important for your sight. You can get it from vegetables, fish, and eggs. So pick up a carrot and get your vitamin A today!

Paragraph B

Vitamin A is important for your sight. You should eat many foods with vitamin A. You can get it from foods such as carrots, eggs, and fish. So pick up a carrot and get your vitamin A today!

Which paragraph is better at getting your attention? Explain your answer.

____

____

B. Read this paragraph. Find the misspelled possessive pronoun and fix it. Then rewrite the beginning of the paragraph, using a question to get the reader's attention.

Brian Jones is the greatest basketball player to come out of our city. In fact, he went to our school! When Brian went to college, his team won the championships. He was even named Most Valuable Player. Now Brian plays in the NBA. If you like basketball, you should be proud of Brian Jones. In fact, be proud of you're school, too!

____

____

Word Choice — Use a quotation or a surprising fact to get your reader's attention.

A. Read each paragraph beginning. Mark the one that uses a quotation or an interesting fact to get the reader's attention.

1. ☐ Making paper airplanes is simple. I have made paper airplanes for many years and can tell you exactly what to do.

☐ Wilbur Wright said, "It is possible to fly without motors, but not without knowledge and skill." He's still right. All you need is a little knowledge and skill to make a great paper airplane.

2. ☐ To keep penguins rescued from oil spills warm, scientists put sweaters on them.

☐ Penguins must be kept warm after they are rescued from oil spills.

B. Read this paragraph. Find the misspelled word and fix it. Then rewrite the beginning of the paragraph, using a quotation or an interesting fact to get the reader's attention.

A honey badger is a type of weasel. Its jaws are very powerful. It often kills and eats snakes in its native African deserts. Even if you are a bee, your not safe from the honey badger! This animal can eat live bees. Its skin is so thick, it can't feel the bees' stings!

____

____

____

____

Start a story by telling about a sudden, unexpected, or mysterious event.

A. Read these personal narratives. Write an *X* next to the one that begins by telling about an unexpected event.

☐ Last Sunday night, I was eating dinner with my mom and grandma, when all of a sudden we heard a huge crash above us! Our upstairs neighbor's foot had come through the ceiling and was dangling above our table! We all jumped up and ran from the kitchen. We were terrified! Later, we found out that there was a water leak. The water had rotted away our ceiling and the neighbor's floor.

☐ There was a leak in my upstairs neighbor's apartment. Our ceiling was rotting, but no one knew about the problem. Then one day, I was eating dinner with my mom and grandma. We heard a huge crash above us! Our upstairs neighbor's foot came right through the ceiling! We jumped up and ran from the kitchen.

B. Read this personal narrative. Find the misspelled words and fix them. Then rewrite the beginning of the narrative so that it starts with an unexpected or mysterious event.

Sometimes you're dog will bark when it senses that an earthquake is coming. That happened once with our dog, Harley. One night the ground started to shake. We had a mild earthquake. Then we figured out why Harley had been barking all day, even though we had taken him for an extra walk. We said to Harley, "Your the only one who knew the earthquake was coming!"

____

____

____

Get your reader's attention with a good beginning.

A. Think of something weird or scary that has happened to you. Use the web to write details about the event.

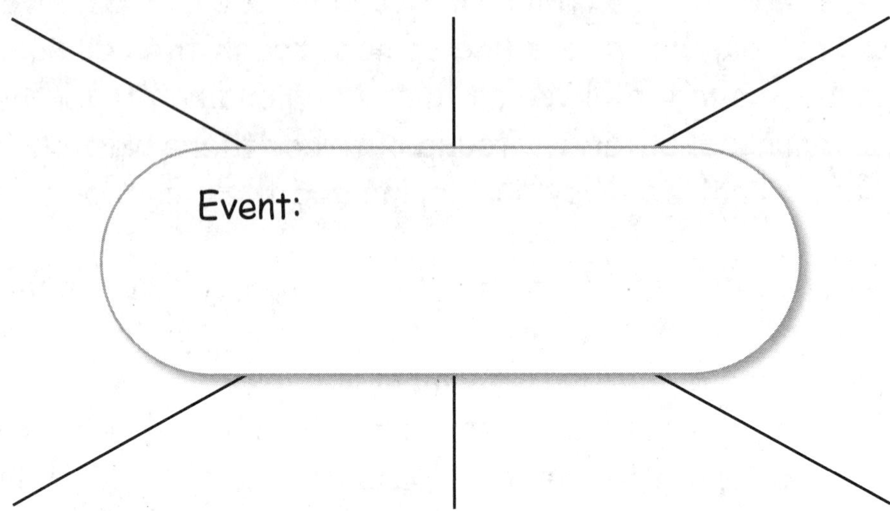

B. Write two good beginnings that would get your reader's attention. Remember these strategies:

- Ask a question.
- Use a quotation.
- Tell an interesting fact.
- Tell about an exciting or mysterious event.

1. ____

   ____

2. ____

   ____

Write a personal narrative about something weird or scary that has happened to you. Include a beginning that will get your reader's attention.

Be sure to use *your* and *you're* correctly.

A run-on sentence is made up of two or more sentences that run together. Run-on sentences make your writing hard to read.

A. Read aloud each paragraph. Then answer the question.

Paragraph 1

Maria's family has Thanksgiving at her grandmother's house every year. Grandma has the biggest table in the family! It can fit turkey, enchiladas, and many more goodies. So, we all bring our favorite dishes and eat a big meal. Then we go for a long walk at the beach.

Paragraph 2

Maria's family has Thanksgiving at her grandmother's house every year because Grandma has the biggest table and it can fit turkey, enchiladas, and many more goodies so we all bring our favorite dishes and eat a big meal then we go for a long walk at the beach.

Why is Paragraph 2 a run-on sentence?

____

____

B. Rewrite each run-on sentence below. Turn it into two smaller sentences.

1. Adam walks fast toward the water the rest of us walk behind him while looking for shells and rocks.

____

____

2. Aunt Sara builds sand castles in the summer once she won money in a contest and bought a bike.

____

____

Sentence Fluency

A rambling sentence has too many *ands, buts,* or *sos.* Fix rambling and run-on sentences by breaking them into smaller sentences.

Read this cause-and-effect paragraph. Find the two run-on and two rambling sentences and underline them. Then rewrite each one, using the correct punctuation to break them up.

Have you ever left out a cold glass of milk only to come back and find that it's become warm and have you ever tried to drink a big mug of hot chocolate quickly before it cooled off in the winter air? Most of us know that liquid won't stay hot or cold for long. But if you put hot soup in a thermos, it will stay warm, a thermos will also keep cold liquid cold how can a thermos do this? It's called radiation! Inside a thermos is a silver mirror, this special kind of mirror can reflect energy. Icy liquid has cold energy so the thermos gives back cold energy and hot liquid has warm energy so the thermos gives back warm energy and that's how a thermos works. The mirror inside a thermos may not be good for combing your hair or checking your teeth, but it can be very useful at lunchtime!

1. ____

____

____

2. ____

____

____

3. ____

____

4. ____

____

Sentence Fluency

Read aloud your writing to check for run-on and rambling sentences.

A. Look at the sequence map for this fantasy story about Juan. Then finish writing the story.

Introduction ⇨ Event ⇨ Turning Point ⇨ Event ⇨ Conclusion

One day, Juan went to the city dump. He found a computer that looked really old. ____

____

____

____

____

____

____

____

____

____

B. Read your story to a partner, pausing after each sentence. Check for run-on and rambling sentences as you read. Then correct any that you find.

Sentence Fluency

Watch out for run-on and rambling sentences as you write.

Choose one of the introductions below. Then write a sentence that tells what happens in each part of the story.

Introduction:

☐ Once upon a time, there was a princess who loved to climb trees. One day, she was climbing a willow tree in the enchanted forest when...

☐ It was a cold, windy day on Planet Azure. Lexi and Vin were riding their scooter-bots across the blue sand when...

☐ Jonah had always wanted a dog, but there was something strange about the little puppy sitting on his doorstep...

Event: ____

____

____

Turning Point: _______________________________________

____

____

Event: ____

____

____

Conclusion: ____

____

____

Write a fantasy story using the sentences you wrote on Day 4.
Add additional sentences to give more details about the story.

Correct any run-on sentences by breaking them into smaller
sentences.

Sentence Fluency

Use a comma and a conjunction (*and, but,* or *or*) to combine two short sentences into one compound sentence.

A. Read this advertisement for a guitar. Underline each compound sentence, and circle its comma and conjunction.

BE A POP STAR WITH YOUR OWN GUITAR!

The Pop Rock Music Store has new guitars in stock. We have almost a hundred, and we want to sell them now! Each guitar comes with five free lessons. Learn to play the hits of the day, or learn to write your own. So, hurry down today to get your new guitar. We may have a lot of them now, but they won't last long!

B. Read each pair of sentences. Use a comma and the conjunction at the end to combine the sentences into one compound sentence.

1. Steven likes to sing. He plays piano. *(and)*

____

____

2. Michelle can play violin. She can dance in the talent show. *(or)*

____

____

3. The other kids want to sing. They don't know a good song. *(but)*

____

____

Sentence Fluency

Use a comma and a conjunction (*and, but,* or *or*) to combine two short sentences into one compound sentence.

A. Read this autobiography. Underline short sentences that could be combined into one compound sentence. Then use a comma and a conjunction to write each new compound sentence on the lines.

> My name is Charlie. I am from Miami. My parents own a bike shop. When I was little, I played in the shop while my parents worked. All of my memories are about riding bikes. We never went to the mall or to the beach. I can't swim fast. I can ride a bike all day! I won my first bike race when I was seven. When I grow up, I want to race more. I could be a pro racer. I could take over the bike shop.

1. ____

   ____

2. ____

   ____

3. ____

   ____

B. Read this description of a person. Find the errors in the compound sentences. Use proofreading marks to correct them.

> Isabella works in the after-school center. She helps with homework, she coaches soccer. She has brown hair and green eyes. Her favorite color is red but don't give her red licorice. She is allergic to candy! You can see Isabella on the playground you can see her in the library. You just won't see her in the candy store!

Sentence Fluency

Use compound sentences in your writing.

Read the Venn diagram. Then write a paragraph that compares and contrasts Earth and Mars. Include at least 3 compound sentences, using a comma and a conjunction.

Conjunctions		
and	but	or

Earth

- 3rd planet from the sun
- takes 365 days to go around the sun
- has animal and plant life

Both

- part of the same solar system
- have ice on their North and South Poles
- have volcanoes

Mars

- 4th planet from the sun
- takes 687 days to go around the sun
- has no animal or plant life
- has the largest volcano in the solar system

____

____

____

____

____

____

____

Use compound sentences in your writing.

Choose two rooms in your school. Write their names in the circles of the Venn diagram. Then fill in the diagram to compare and contrast the rooms.

Here are some things to think about:

- the furniture
- what's on the walls
- what you do in the rooms
- who is in the rooms

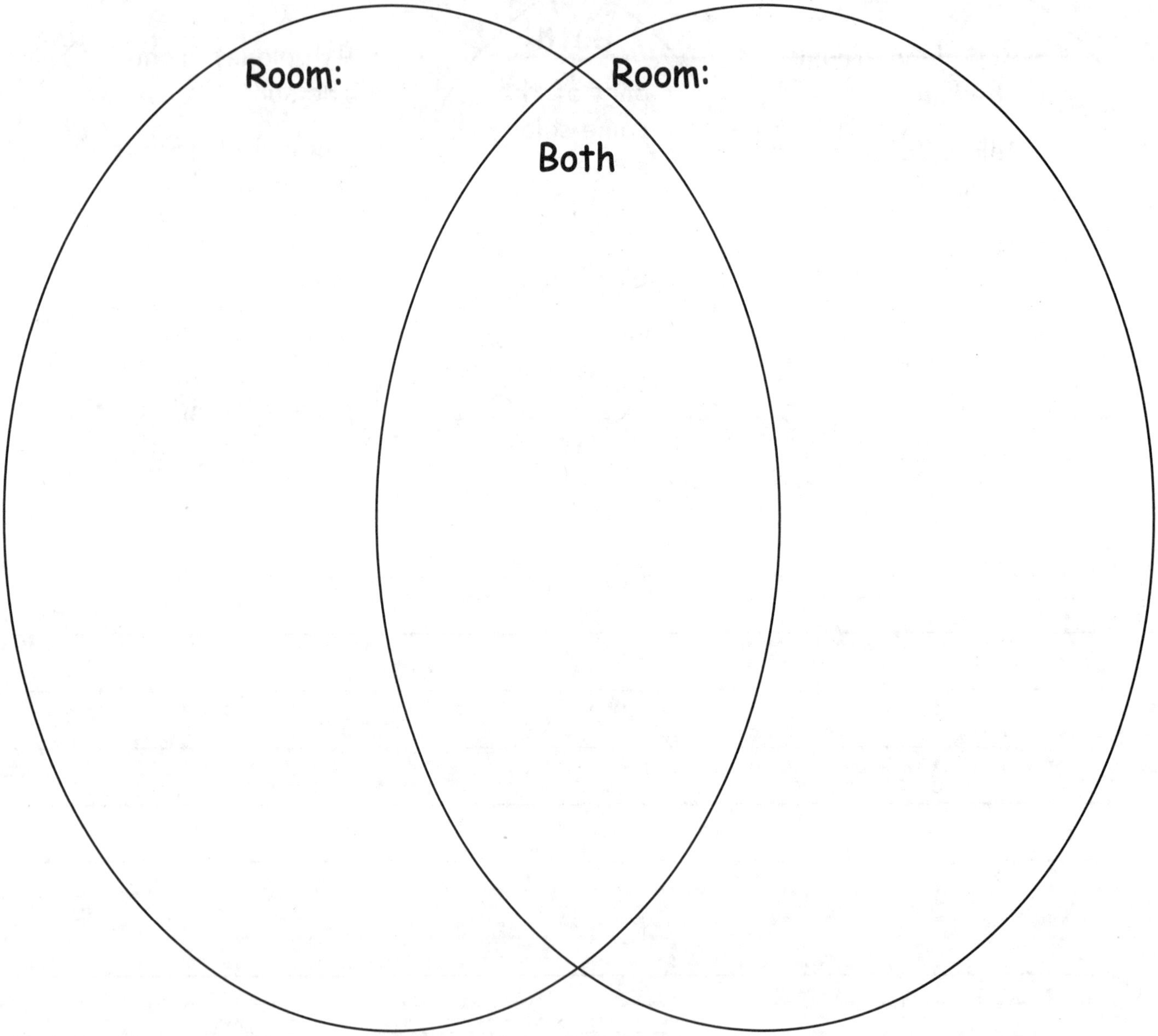

Room:

Room:

Both

Write a paragraph that compares and contrasts two rooms in your school. Include at least three compound sentences. Make sure each one has a comma and the conjunction *and*, *but*, or *or*.

You can combine two simple sentences into a complex sentence, using certain conjunctions.

A. Read this thank-you note. Find each sentence that contains a conjunction from the box. Circle the conjunction. Underline the two sentences that it combines.

Conjunctions	
before	if
because	while

Dear Uncle Isaiah,

   Thank you for my drawing pad and colored pencils. I like them because I am learning how to draw. I want to try drawing before I learn to paint. You can see my drawings if you visit this summer. I could even draw a picture of you while you are here.

                    Love,

                    Shelby

B. Read each pair of sentences. Choose the best conjunction from the box to combine the sentences into one sentence. Then write the new sentence.

Conjunctions		
after	unless	while

1. Gabe played video games. He read his comics.

____

2. Barkly doesn't get a bone. He rolls over.

____

3. You do the dishes. I vacuum and dust.

____

Add variety to your writing by using complex sentences that start with a conjunction.

A. Read each sentence. Underline the two simple sentences that were combined. Circle the conjunction.

Conjunctions	
although	once
before	when

1. Before Chloe goes to bed, she always brushes her teeth.

2. Once Luis has finished his dinner, he may go outside.

3. Although it rained, we had a good time on the camping trip.

4. When the bell rang, everyone hurried into their classrooms.

B. Read each pair of sentences. Choose the best conjunction from the box to combine the sentences. Then write the new sentence, starting with the conjunction. Remember to use a comma between the combined sentences.

Conjunctions	
If	Once
While	Whenever

1. Melissa wins the spelling bee. She will be the Spelling Champion.

____

____

2. Carlos makes a funny face. The baby laughs.

____

____

3. You are slicing the carrots. I will chop the onion.

____

____

4. I clean up my mess. I'll start my homework.

____

____

Add variety to your writing by using complex sentences.

Read the timeline. It shows events in the life of Hank Aaron, a famous baseball player. Use the timeline to write a short paragraph about Hank Aaron. Use the conjunctions in the box to write at least three complex sentences.

1934	Henry Louis "Hank" Aaron is born in Mobile, Alabama.
1948	Hank sees Jackie Robinson, the first African American to play in the Major Leagues. He decides his dream is to play in the Majors, too.
1954	Hank plays his first major-league game for the Milwaukee Braves. He scores a home run the first time at bat!
1974	Hank bats his 715th home run, breaking Babe Ruth's record!
1976	Hank retires from baseball, having set many records.
2002	President George W. Bush awards Hank the Medal of Freedom.

Conjunctions			
after	because	until	while
although	before	when	

Sentence Fluency

Add variety to your writing by using complex sentences.

A. Think of a famous person whom you admire. Research the person's life, using the Internet, books, or magazines. Then use the timeline below to write down six important events in his or her life.

The Life of _______________________________

B. Write two complex sentences to describe events on your timeline. Begin one sentence with a conjunction.

____

____

____

____

____

Write a short biography of someone you admire, using the timeline you made on Day 4. Include at least three complex sentences in your biography. Be sure to use conjunctions and commas correctly.

When you start every sentence the same way, your writing can sound boring.

A. Read Kaylee's journal entries. Answer the question. Then find and fix the interjection that needs correct capitalization and punctuation.

June 10, 2009

We met a new kid in Drama Club today. Elijah is from Alaska. Elijah is very tall. Elijah wants to play Paul Bunyan in our school play. We made sets for the play. We went home. We had meatloaf for dinner. Yuck!

June 10, 2009

Today we met a new kid in Drama Club. Elijah is from Alaska. He is very tall! Since we are doing Paul Bunyan for the school play, Elijah wants to play Paul. After we made sets for the play, it was time to go home. Do you know what was for dinner? We had meatloaf. yuck

Which journal entry sounds better? What is the difference between the sentence beginning in each one?

____

____

B. Read the short paragraph. Rewrite the paragraph so the sentences do not begin in the same way.

Cynthia wrote a story. Cynthia's story is called "Catch That Rat!" Cynthia wants Greg to draw pictures for her story.

____

____

____

Sentence Fluency

Look for sentences that begin in the same way.
Rewrite them so your writing doesn't sound boring.

Read each paragraph. Write an *X* next to the paragraph with sentence beginnings that need to be improved. Then rewrite that paragraph on the lines. Try beginning the sentences in different ways. Also, fix the interjection that needs correct punctuation.

☐ Sabrina's family went to the Neighborhood Cleanup Day. There was a trash pickup contest. Quickly, Sabrina picked up trash in the park and in the schoolyard. She picked up so much trash that she won the contest! Overall, the neighborhood collected twenty bags of trash and recycling. Wow, that's a lot of litter! It's hard to believe there's so much junk hanging around the neighborhood.

☐ For the summer, Henry went to Arizona. It was hot. It was fun. First, Henry met a lot of relatives. Then, he visited the Grand Canyon. Then, there was a party for his birthday. Then, there was a giant thunderstorm. Henry had never seen anything like it. "Yikes look at the lightning and clouds!" he shouted. His cousins laughed. They were used to the storms. They went to the movies a few times. They played a lot and rode bikes around town.

____

____

____

____

____

____

____

Revise your sentences so they begin in different ways.
Your writing will sound more interesting.

Read this thank-you letter. Look for sentences that begin in the same way. Then rewrite the body of the letter, revising the sentences so they begin in different ways. Also, fix any interjections that need correct capitalization and punctuation.

Dear Kate,

    Thank you for giving me your old skateboard. The board is perfect. The board is just what I wanted. If I didn't have this board, I would have to borrow Miranda's! Miranda's board is pink. Miranda's board has flowers on it. ick Soon, I'll get some stickers for it. Soon, I'll also get a new helmet.

    I want to try out the board soon. I want to go skateboarding with you! Patrick can come, too. Patrick is good at going down hills. The first time I went down a hill, I crashed! Whoa, Nelly!

                Your friend,
                Nelly

____

____

____

____

____

____

____

____

If you begin your sentences in different ways, your writing will sound more interesting.

A. Think of a gift someone has given you. Complete the web, describing the gift and the person who gave it to you.

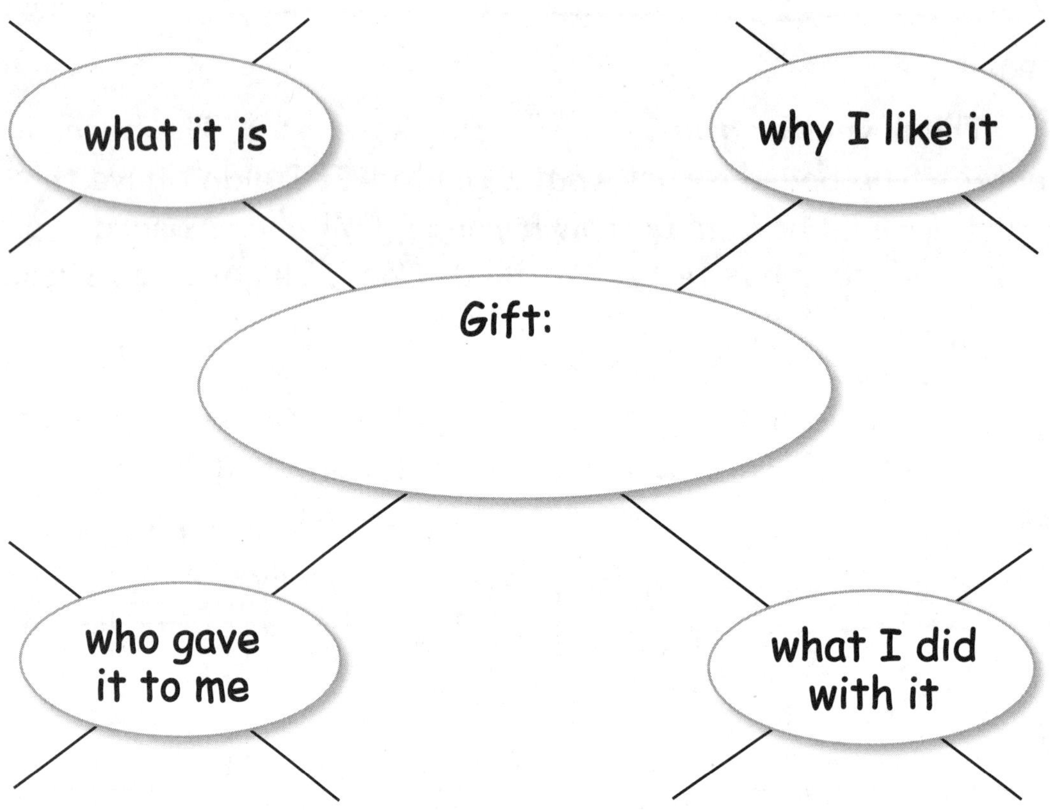

B. Write one sentence about the gift. Use an interjection in your sentence.

Interjections		
cool	hey	oops
wow	yikes	whoa

____

____

Write a thank-you note for a gift you have received. Remember to begin your sentences in different ways.

Include at least one interjection on its own or at the beginning of a sentence.

Use statements, questions, and exclamations in the same paragraph to make your writing sound interesting.

Read these book reviews. Find and correct each sentence fragment. Then answer the questions.

Book Review A

Charlotte's Web is about two animals. It was written by E.B. White. Wilbur is a pig. Charlotte is a spider. Wilbur's owner wants to kill him. Charlotte tries to save him. She writes messages in her webs. You should read this book. You will see what happens. Is happy and sad.

Book Review B

Charlotte's Web is by E.B. White. The main characters are Wilbur and Charlotte. Wilbur is a friendly pig, and Charlotte is a clever spider. When Wilbur's owner wants to turn him into a Christmas ham, Charlotte tries to save Wilbur. She writes messages in her webs! Clever messages about him. So, what happens? Read the book and find out! The ending is both happy and sad.

1. Which review has statements, questions, and exclamations? ____

2. Which review has only statements? ____

3. Which review sounds better while reading it aloud? Why?

____

____

Sentence Fluency

Use short and long sentences in the same paragraph. Different sentence lengths help your writing flow.

A. Read this paragraph. Then rewrite the paragraph so it flows better. Combine some of the short, choppy sentences into longer sentences.

> I love mangoes. I eat fresh mangoes. I eat mango ice cream. I eat mango salsa. One day, I wanted a mango. Aunt Molly said, "No." I took it. Aunt Molly wasn't looking. It wasn't ripe. It was hard! I dropped the heavy thing on my foot. Ouch! That hurt.

____

____

____

____

____

____

B. Read each sentence. Write *F* if the sentence is a fragment. Write *C* if the sentence is complete. Then choose two fragments. Turn each one into a complete sentence. Write the new sentences on the lines.

1. Kelly sat. _____

2. A lot of cute, furry rabbits. _____

3. Grandpa Miguel lives there. _____

4. In a house in the country. _____

5. New Sentence: _______________________________________

____

6. New Sentence: _______________________________________

____

Sentence Fluency

Include different kinds of sentences for a smooth-sounding paragraph.

Read this description of an event. Then rewrite the paragraph, fixing the sentence fragments and improving the flow. Use these strategies for revising the sentences:

- Break up run-on sentences.
- Combine short, choppy sentences into compound or complex sentences.
- Use both short and long sentences.
- Use questions and exclamations.

It was the last day of school. It was exciting. The classes gathered in the gym. Principal Lee gave out awards. Victor won the Perfect Attendance award. He came to school. Every day of the year. Zoe won Best at Math. Paul won Best Reader. We had silly awards, too. I won Best at Recess. Everybody laughed. Later, we had games and they were on the playground and I saw Alicia win the blue ribbon. For the jump rope contest. The last bell rang. We yelled, "See you next year!"

____

____

____

____

____

____

____

____

Include different kinds of sentences for a smooth-sounding paragraph.

A. Think of a special day you had at school. Fill in the chart with details that describe the day.

Special School Day: _______________________________________

Saw	
Heard	
Smelled	
Tasted	
Touched	

B. Use the details from Activity A to write complete sentences. Follow the prompts.

1. Write a long sentence about the day.

____

____

2. Write a short sentence about the day.

____

3. Write an exclamation about the day.

____

4. Write a question you could ask about the day.

____

Write a description of a special school day. Include different types of sentences, and begin your sentences in different ways. Make sure your writing flows and that you haven't used any sentence fragments.

Voice Some writing has an exciting voice.

A. Fill in the phrases that help make this narrative exciting.

Word Box		
searching wildly	surprised everyone	good friends
cheered loudly	getting nervous	

Kittens, Kittens, Kittens!
by Rosie

Mrs. Hornblower's cat, Lucy Lou, _________________________

with six kittens yesterday! It was quite a morning, because

Mrs. Hornblower is our bus driver. Lucy Lou was hiding in the

closet, and Mrs. H was _________________________ for her.

While we were worried for Mrs. H, we were _________________________

about being very late for school!

Later, Mrs. Hornblower said she was sorry for making us

tardy. And everyone _________________________ when she

announced, "All my _________________________ on Bus 83 may

help name the kittens! And if you want a kitten of your own,

you can ask your parents to call me!"

B. What do you think Mrs. Hornblower might say about her day?
Write two sentences in an exciting style.

____

____

Voice Some writing has a playful voice. It makes the writing fun to read.

A. Read Riley's playful narrative about the day she was late for school.

Late for School
by Riley

This morning I waited for the bus. I waited, and I waited, and I waited. Then Grandma told me Alejandro's mom had phoned. She said that our bus driver, Mrs. Hornblower, was late for work because she was going crazy looking for her cat, Lucy Lou. After searching her entire house, Mrs. H finally found little Lucy Lou snug as a bug in a rug, snoozing away in Mrs. Hornblower's sun hat on top of a big blue beach blanket. Lucy Lou had a surprise for Mrs. H—six new baby kittens! Now, I have one question:
Will my teacher believe me when I have to say,
That the Cat in the Hat made me late on this day?

B. How did Riley make her writing fun to read?
Write an example of each way listed below.

1. Repeated words:

   ____

2. Amusing words:

   ____

3. Words that begin with the same letter:

   ____

4. The last two lines are a _______________________

Voice   Some writing has a formal, serious-sounding voice.

A. Alejandro wrote a letter to his teacher, explaining why he didn't have his homework. He used formal language and made sure to include important facts that his teacher would take seriously. Underline the facts and circle examples of formal language.

> Dear Mrs. Garcia,
>
> I must apologize for not having my homework today. I would like to explain what happened. This morning, I stood at the bus stop for a long time. Finally, I went back into the house and my mom called the school. We learned the bus driver was late getting to work. Just then, the bus honked, and I ran out the door without my backpack! That is why I do not have my homework today.
>
> As you know, I have brought in my homework every day this month. I can promise you I will bring the missing homework tomorrow. May I still receive homework points for it?
>
> Your student,
>
> Alejandro

B. Pretend you are Alejandro's mother. Write two sentences to Mrs. Garcia in support of Alejandro. Use a serious style.

____

____

____

C. Write *can* or *may* to complete the sentences.

1. _____________ I go to the library?

2. I _____________ return these books for you.

Voice Write in an exciting, funny, or serious voice.

Think of a school morning when some events didn't go as usual.
It can be real or imaginary. Fill in the events in this flowchart.
Then choose a writing style for your story by checking a box.

Writing Style: ☐ Serious ☐ Funny ☐ Exciting

Event 1

Event 2

Event 3

Event 4

Event 5

Write about a school morning when things didn't go as usual.
Use the events and style you chose on Day 4.

Be sure to use *can* and *may* correctly.

To persuade someone, match your voice to your purpose and audience.

A. Two students wrote to the governor of their state with a special request. Which voice matches the purpose and audience best? Which one is more likely to persuade the governor? Then find and correct the double negative.

1. Dear Governor,

   Have you heard about "I Love to Write" Day? It is a special day to encourage everyone, young and old, to write. I learned about it from my fourth-grade teacher. Last year, nine governors named November 15 as a special day in their states. They recognized that it is important for all people to become better writers. So, I am writing to you with a great idea! Why not celebrate "I Love to Write" Day in our state next year? It would be fun for everyone. Thank you for considering my request.

2. Hi!

   I'm a 4th-grader in Mr. Marshall's class. Let me tell you about "I Love to Write" Day. Last Thursday, we had a lot of fun writing poems in our class. But "I Love to Write" Day is for everybody, not just kids. There isn't no day like this in our state yet. You should make it a big deal all over the state next year. How about it? That would be sweet! Thanks!

B. Match the formal language in the first letter to the informal language in the second.

Informal Language	Formal Language
Hi!	_______________________
not just kids	_______________________
make it a big deal	_______________________
That would be sweet!	_______________________
Thanks!	_______________________

Voice — To persuade your readers, speak directly to them, give reasons that support your ideas, and show emotion.

A. A student wrote an article for his school newsletter. Help him proofread it for double negatives. Use proofreading marks to take out a negative word, and write a word from the box in its place.

Word Box
any   anyone   anything

Cereal Day Fights Hunger
by Cody

You can help fight hunger in our town! Every morning, some children don't have nothing to eat for breakfast. We can help those kids by giving to the Food Pantry. The Food Pantry helps families. It is a place where people can go to get food when they do not have no money to buy it.

Next Friday is Cereal Day. Just bring one box of cereal to school. It doesn't cost a lot, and it's easy to carry in your backpack. Mrs. Young will take all the cereal to the Food Pantry. Then there will be lots to give away.

Don't forget your cereal box next Friday! We can help to make sure there won't be nobody who goes hungry.

B. Write two sentences that would persuade your friends to take part in Cereal Day.

____

____

____

Voice Bring out your voice by clearly stating your opinion.

A. Decide how you would answer each question. Write a strong
opinion statement and one reason to support that opinion.

1. Your school has been given $10,000 dollars. The entire amount may be spent
on new gym equipment, new art supplies, <u>or</u> new library books. Which one
should the money be spent on?

____

____

2. Should your class go on a field trip to a science museum, a play, <u>or</u>
an aquarium?

____

____

3. Should students be allowed to have their cellphones in the classroom?

____

____

B. Read these sentences. Use proofreading marks to correct the
double negatives.

1. We have not been on no field trips this year.

2. I've never been to no aquarium.

3. Nobody said nothing about going to a zoo.

Voice   Use your voice when you want to be persuasive.

Read these community service project ideas. Choose one project to persuade your class to do. Write your opinion statement in the box. Then write a reason to do that project in each circle.

Community Service Projects:

☐   Volunteer at a wildlife rescue center. Help birds, amphibians, and small mammals that are hurt or sick.

☐   Hold a book drive to collect new and used books. Donate the books to schools or libraries that need them.

☐   Raise money to build wells in Africa. Hold fundraisers to collect the money.

Opinion Statement:

Write a paragraph to persuade your class to perform the community service project you chose on Day 4.

Be sure your sentences do not contain double negatives.

A story can be told from different points of view. Your point of view affects the voice you use when you write.

Travis and Aunt Heather each wrote a personal narrative about the same situation. Read the narratives. Then answer the questions.

Travis

My birthday is going to be a real bummer. First, I found out that Mom and Dad have to work all day, so I'll be spending the day with Aunt Heather. But then I saw her at the grocery store last night.

"What are we going to do for my birthday?" I asked her.

"Umm, I don't know," Aunt Heather said. She frowned a little bit.

"But Mom and Dad said we could do something really fun!"

"I know, but I think I caught a cold," she said with a sniffle.

1. What does Travis think will happen on his birthday?

   ____

2. What kind of voice does he use in his narrative? ________________________

Aunt Heather

I ran into Travis at the grocery store today! He asked me what we were doing for his birthday.

"Umm, I don't know," I told him as I tried not to smile.

"Mom and Dad said we could do something really fun," he whined.

"I know, but I think I caught a cold." I faked a sniffle. I think he believed me! I can't wait until Saturday when Travis finds out we're having a surprise birthday party for him!

3. What does Aunt Heather know will happen on Travis's birthday?

   ____

4. What kind of voice does she use in her narrative? ________________________

Voice Be creative by telling a story from a different point of view.

A. Look at the pictures. Read the sentences.

Kristen finds a shiny marble.

The marble falls out of her pocket.

Eddie finds his missing marble.

He puts it back in his collection.

B. Imagine the story from the marble's point of view. Imagine it is telling the story to another marble. Finish this conversation between the marbles. Remember to start a new paragraph each time someone new speaks.

"Boy, am I glad to be back!" said the striped marble.
"Where have you been?" asked a white marble.

____

____

____

____

____

____

Voice   Use voice to emphasize a character's point of view.

A. Read this version of "The Little Red Hen." It is told from Hen's point of view. Use the paragraph symbol (¶) to mark where there should be a new paragraph. Then answer the question.

> Once, I found some grains of wheat. I wanted to plant the wheat and make bread. So I went to my good friend, Pig. "Will you help me plant the wheat?" I asked. "Sorry, but I can't," he said. I also asked for help baking the bread. Pig couldn't help me with that, either. Well, now that I've tired myself out and baked the bread, guess who wants a piece? Pig, of course! But I decided to keep it for myself because I was the one who worked hard on it. This bread is mine—ALL MINE!

What voice does Hen use when explaining her point of view? Give an example from the story to support your answer.

____

____

B. Read Pig's version of the story. Rewrite it with a stronger voice, having Pig defend himself with more excitement. Include at least one line of dialogue.

> Hen is my friend. But she won't share her bread. One day, she asked for help planting the wheat. I said I couldn't help her. I also couldn't help her with the baking. I had important homework to do.

____

____

____

____

____

Tell a story from a different point of view.
Use the character's voice.

A. Think of a folk tale or fairy tale you know. Write the name of the main character. Then write the name of another character who could tell the story.

Name of Folk Tale: _______________________________________

Main Character: _______________________________________

Other Character: _______________________________________

B. Think about your other character's point of view. Answer the questions.

1. How would your character see the story differently from the main character? Would his or her attitude or feelings be different? Give an example.

____

____

____

____

Example: _______________________________________

____

____

2. What kind of voice(s) would your character use to tell the story?

____

____

____

Voice

Retell a famous tale from another character's point of view. Use voice to emphasize the character's attitudes and feelings. Include dialogue in your story. Be sure to begin a new paragraph each time someone new speaks.

Use rhyming words and images in poems to describe your subject in your own voice.

A. Read the poem. Find words that rhyme at the ends of the lines. Underline the words. Then circle the letters that spell the vowel sound.

Who Has Seen the Wind?
by Christina Rossetti

Who has seen the wind?

Neither I nor you:

But when the leaves hang trembling

The wind is passing through.

Who has seen the wind?

Neither you nor I:

But when the trees bow down their heads

The wind is passing by.

B. "Who Has Seen the Wind?" uses images to describe something invisible—the wind. Look at the chart below. For each invisible thing, write an image that can be used to describe it. Then think of two other invisible things and images to describe them.

Something You Can't See	Image
1. music	
2. winter	
3.	
4.	

You can copy the style and pattern of a poem, but use your own ideas.

A. Read this limerick by Edward Lear. Underline the rhyming words.

> There was a Young Lady whose chin,
>
> Resembled the point of a pin;
>
> So she had it made sharp,
>
> And purchased a harp,
>
> And played several tunes with her chin.

B. Complete these limericks with your own ideas. Remember to use the proper end rhyme.

> Today is the worst kind of day.
>
> The skies are cold and gray.
>
> There's nothing to do.
>
> I'm bored and I'm blue.
>
> _______________________________________
>
> There once was a young man named Sam,
>
> Who was always caught in a jam.
>
> _______________________________________
>
> _______________________________________
>
> That's the last we saw of poor Sam.

Use your voice to say something in an interesting or different way.

A. Brad wrote an acrostic poem about his shoes. Read the poem. Underline the rhyming words at the ends of the lines. Then answer the question.

Shoe
by Brad

Strings, stitches, and leather
Hold my shoes together.
Only, now that I get taller,
Each toe starts to holler!

What is Brad saying about his shoes?

____

B. Audrey wrote an acrostic poem about her shoes. However, it doesn't make sense. Try rewriting Audrey's poem so it has a main idea and rhymes.

Shoe
by Audrey

Sneakers on my feet,
How they are complete.
Oh, a sneaker's cool,
Especially the golden rule.

S____

H____

O____

E____

Use your own words to plan an acrostic poem about yourself.

Write the letters of your name in the boxes. Next to each letter, write words or phrases that begin with that letter.

Letters **Words and Phrases**

Write a rhyming acrostic poem about yourself.

Be sure your rhyming words make sense with the rest of the poem.

Interest your reader by showing who you really are.
Use your unique voice to explain your feelings.

A. Read what each student says. Choose the quotation that is more interesting. Underline the details that explain the character's feelings.

B. Write a sentence about something you love to do. Use your own unique voice.

____

____

C. Reread the quotations in Activity A. Find the three different word pairs that could be made into contractions. Write them on the lines. Then write the contractions for those words.

	Word Pairs	Contractions
1.		
2.		
3.		

Write honestly. Use your unique writing voice to let your readers get to know the real you.

Read each situation and complete the sentence. Be sure to use your own unique voice.

1. If I won the Student of the Year award, I'd say:

2. If someone stole my lunch money, I'd say:

3. If I told my favorite joke, I'd say:

4. If my friend was sick, I'd say:

Voice   Use your unique voice to tell about personal experiences.

Draw a comic strip that tells about a personal experience you've had. Use the ideas in the box to think of a good topic. Then draw what happened in the boxes.

- Use a speech balloon to show what was said.
- Use a thought bubble to show what was thought.

Topic Ideas

a funny moment • a scary moment

an embarrassing moment • being proud of yourself

meeting a new friend • winning or losing a game

1

2

3

4

Voice   Use your unique voice to tell about personal experiences.

If you had to write a journal entry about how this year has been, what would you tell about? Answer the questions to help you think of ideas.

1. What was the best thing that happened this year? What was good about it?

2. What was the worst thing that happened this year? What was bad about it?

3. Name three things you've done this year. Use a contraction in your answer.

4. If you could live this year over again, what would you do differently?
   Use *I've* or *I'd* in your answer.

Voice

Write a journal entry about the best and worst parts of this year. Write about what you have done and what you would do differently.

Be sure to spell contractions correctly.

Dear Journal,

Proofreading Marks

Mark	Meaning	Example
ℰ	Take this out (delete).	I love ~~so~~ to read.
⊙	Add a period.	It was late⊙
≡	Make this a capital letter.	First prize went to m̲aria.
/	Make this a lowercase letter.	We saw a ₿lack ₵at.
———	Fix the spelling.	This is our ~~hause~~ house.
⌃	Add a comma.	Goodnight⌃ Mom.
⌄	Add an apostrophe.	That⌄s Lil⌄s bike.
⌄⌄	Add quotation marks.	⌄Come in, he said.⌄
! ? ⌃ ⌃	Add an exclamation point or a question mark.	Help⌃! Can you help me⌃?
⌃̄	Add a hyphen.	I've read three⌃fourths of the book.
⌣	Close the space.	Foot⌣ball is fun.
⌃	Add a word or letter.	The⌃ red pen is mine.
———	Underline the words.	We read <u>Old Yeller</u>.
⌃	Add a colon.	Alex arrived at 4⌃00.

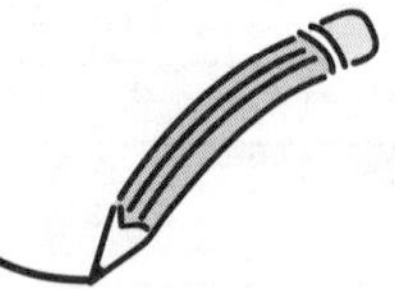